PRESSURE OFF

PRESSURE OFF

Learning to embrace the gift of God's grace

Monique Thomas

FORM

First published in Great Britain in 2023

Society for Promoting Christian Knowledge
Suite 101, The Record Hall,
16–16A Baldwins Gardens,
London EC1N 7RJ
www.spck.org.uk

British Library Cataloguing-in-Publication Data
A catalogue record for this book is available from the British Library

ISBN 978–0–281–08769–3
eBook ISBN 978–0–281–08770–9

1 3 5 7 9 10 8 6 4 2

First printed in Great Britain by Clays Limited, Bungay, NR35 1ED

eBook by Typeset by Fakenham Prepress Solutions, Fakenham, Norfolk, NR21 8NL

Produced on paper from sustainable sources.

Connect with Monique on Instagram: https://www.instagram.com/itsmoniquethomas

Contents

Introduction   1

1 Pressure off productivity   14

2 Pressure off perfection   30

3 Pressure off singleness   43

4 Pressure off purity   55

5 Pressure off marriage   67

6 Pressure off parenting   81

7 Pressure off power   96

8 Pressure off prosperity   111

Conclusion: Pressure on   127

Introduction

When was the last time you were able to breathe *deeply?*

Let's try it now.

Find a comfortable position, place your hand on your stomach and feel it expand as we inhale and exhale through the nose…

In, 2, 3, 4 and out, 2, 3, 4…

In, 2, 3, 4 and out, 2, 3, 4…

In, 2, 3, 4 and out, 2, 3, 4…

In, 2, 3, 4 and out, 2, 3, 4.

It's incredible what a few deep breaths can accomplish. As we inhaled, our body was being oxygenated, activating the parasympathetic nervous system that shifts us into the 'rest and digest' mode. It's telling our brain that we're *safe*. When we're stressed our sympathetic system automatically kicks us into 'fight or flight' mode, marked by shallowness of breath and an increased heart rate. Wouldn't it be great if we could just *breathe* our way to permanent peace? If we could still every storm within as we find five minutes to simply be?

Chances are if you're reading this book, you also feel the pervasive sense that the tides of life are overwhelming us. A recent study in Great Britain reported that more than 70% of those surveyed felt unable to cope because of stress at some point during the year.[1] Wherever you look, the statistics reveal that mental health challenges are growing more prevalent and complex, even in the innocent minds of our children.[2] From financial troubles and relationship issues to living with the effects of an increasingly divided society, it's a worldwide trend, but often a lonely and isolating experience. Of course, it is far too easy to play the victim in conversations about pressure and our global conscience helps to bring some much-needed perspective. It may not be the stress born of tsunamis, persecution or war but it does little to minimise the relative pressure that is being experienced in even the most privileged societies today.

In his book, *Status Anxiety*, philosopher Alain de Botton argues that 'anxiety is the handmaiden of contemporary ambition'.[3] From money goals and family goals to career goals and the piling expectations of others, sometimes we can't ascertain if we are the cause of the strain or experiencing the effect of something 'out there'. Pressure has become a part of who we are, and we have become so familiar with unhealthy levels of it that we don't always recognise its presence until it hits us in the face. Even then, we often only treat the *symptoms* because the root, if we can find it, is too painful or too hard to address. It's hurting the way we relate to ourselves, each other and our environment. Many of us know that we desperately need a better way.

> Are you tired? Worn out? Burned out on religion? Come to me. Get away with me and you'll recover your life. I'll show you how to take a real rest. Walk with me and work with me – watch how I do it. Learn the unforced rhythms of grace. I won't lay anything heavy or ill-fitting on you. Keep company with me and you'll learn to live freely and lightly.
> (Matthew 11:28–30, *The Message*)

I believe that this better Way is Jesus. For the worn out he invites us to *come to him* so that he can teach us how to *recover our lives* and *live freely*. Not in a mythical sense but as an embodied reality. His gospel, reflected in his life and teachings, provides a compelling message that responds to the deeply seated unrest that is present in our world today. So why are fewer Westerners choosing to identify as Christians?

In England and Wales, according to the latest census data the percentage of those identifying as Christian has fallen from 71% in

2001, to 59% in 2011 and 46% in 2021.[4] While immigrant communities significantly help to keep Christianity alive in Britain, in the US, according to the Pew Research Center, 'If recent trends in religious switching continue, Christians could make up less than half of the US population within a few decades.'[5] Speaking to *The Observer*, Abby Day, Professor of Race, Faith and Culture at Goldsmiths, University of London commented that: 'Religion tends to be transmitted within families. But many baby boomers, who were largely brought up by people who went to church, dramatically broke with that.'[6] She goes on to say that, 'Post-Christians are motivated by ethics concerning gender and sexual equality, social justice, climate change and compassion. The churches failed to deliver on those moral issues and so lost moral authority.' For some, the Bible is an outdated rule book, God a disappointed Father and the church family a crowd of acquaintances whose opinions need filtering.

In faith circles we expect great things from God which sometimes results in us placing too high demands on ourselves *and* others, causing those inside the Church to feel weighed down and those outside the Church to assume Jesus must be hard work. Although we claim to have the gift of God's grace, as Christians we often fall victim to the same pressures as wider society. We're also obsessed with perfection and an unhealthy view of holiness divorces us from the messiness of our humanity. Yet Jesus' entry into our world, his life and death, couldn't be grubbier – born in a manger and hung on an old rugged cross. So why do we subconsciously buy into the myth that we have to have it all together? His mission was to set the captives free, yet our commitment to the Church and what appears necessary for spiritual growth, can leave us feeling enslaved to an oversubscribed spiritual 'to-do' list that demands more, more, more. We're called to love each other deeply as a witness to the world – so, for many of us, why does it feel like we can be more real and are more accepted beyond the four walls of our churches? If the gospel is truly the doorway to freedom, why do we feel trapped in cycles of shame and striving? Sadly, for many of us, our Christian communities are the place where we feel the *most* pressure.

My story

'Lord, I don't know if you're real but if you are I want you to show me.' That was my prayer at the altar of a National Youth Convention before I fell down in the Spirit and opened my eyes underneath a chair on the front row. What just happened?! I was seventeen and pretty green when it came to Christianity, and though I left that weekend with doubts, I'd had an experience that I couldn't shake. Around the same time, my school friend invited me to her church, where crying through the message and responding to the altar call in tears became a weekly event. I later grew to understand it was the healing work of the Holy Spirit. My values were changing and so was my outlook on life. At seventeen, I was opened up to a whole new world...

...And at nineteen, I fell pregnant.

It seemed the worst thing that could happen in my new-found community. Terrified of the consequences, I decided to have an abortion in secret. In my gut it felt wrong, yet having a child at nineteen felt wrong too. And though I thought that nobody knowing about the abortion would enable me to escape public condemnation, the reality was that the silent shame was breaking me. Whenever there was a baby dedication at church I cried and every time we prayed for a woman desperate to conceive, I wanted the ground to swallow me up. I feared the judgement of God but nevertheless, I still continued to have unprotected sex (in my mind if I planned to use protection, that would mean I was planning to have sex – but who was I kidding?) while still serving at my church out of a desire to please him. I was stuck – but this was my own doing. I wanted help, but who could I talk to?

4

After almost two years, I opened up to a close friend who encouraged me to speak to our pastor. I wanted to suss her out to see if I could really trust her, so initially just shared that I was having sex, then seeing that she was kind and wise, I later told her about the abortion. To my surprise, she didn't judge and criticise but she helped me to face myself and then led me on a journey of restoring my relationship with God. Not because he had turned away from me, but rather that I had felt so unworthy that I couldn't truly turn to him. Pastor Sandra saw the best in me. She made time and encouraged me to be all that I could be. Sometimes I couldn't understand what it was exactly that she was seeing, but I felt loved, accepted and *safe*. Her entry into my life was a game changer. I began to understand the value of being vulnerable before God. The power of confession with a trusted other, the importance of repentance and how breaking the silence disarms our shame.

I don't share this story as a piece of pro-choice or pro-life propaganda (I sincerely recognise how sensitive and inflammatory the topic of abortion is), but rather to show that fear and the pressures surrounding it were silencing me. However, through my confession, instead of condemning me, the Lord graciously healed one of the greatest sources of pressure and pain in my life when there was nothing that I could do to undo the past.

During my twenties, I continued to grow in many ways as a believer. I loved the Bible and found much comfort and direction in reading it. I laughed, danced, sang and prayed in the Spirit but eventually, my experience of Christianity stopped making sense. My passion for the Lord felt like it had waned, and I was unfulfilled with my Sunday experience too. To the frustration of those close to me I started questioning everything. Why do we do things like this? Why are we praying for that? Why do we say this? I stopped standing in church, I stopped raising my hands and I stopped saying 'amen'.

One Sunday during the preaching I slipped off the back row in frustration, headed out the back door and bumped into a friend. Unaware of what I was going through she said,

> Oh Mon, I've been meaning to message you for a few weeks now… The Lord told me to tell you that he's taking you back to undo everything you've learnt so he can refine you but he doesn't want you to get discouraged in the process.

I didn't show it but I was blown away by how timely this word was and overwhelmed by God's kindness in sending it. He was the one behind this restlessness that left me wanting! The unsettling I felt was not wrong, it was an invitation from him to draw closer.

Today this testimony continues to give me permission and confidence to wrestle with my faith and I hope it does the same for you. Questions are necessary for understanding, they help us mature and build strong foundations. When we halt our exploration or isolate it from our relationship with God, we discourage the challenge that leads to growth, but I've learnt that when we involve him in our seeking it leads to revelation and peace. Instead of silencing me, the Lord graciously encouraged my searching when I felt the pressure to conform. And I've experienced his empowering grace through every stage of my journey since then: as a school teacher, a tutor in prison, in my years serving the local church, hosting events, writing and performing as a music artist, throughout my studies, in being a wife, daughter and friend, and a mother to three beautiful boys. I don't know your story, your joys or your pain, but whatever the cause of your pressure, Jesus still says, 'Come.'

Our story

Are you feeling the strain? Do you feel burned out? The good news is that the grace of God is both redemptive and restoring, it is a free gift of undeserved *favour* and *forgiveness* for sinners (Romans 5:15), and it is also *power* for living (2 Corinthians 12:9–10). Jesus' descent into our broken existence and his message of salvation offers hope for our weary hearts. His unquenchable love liberates and invites us into his kingdom, no strings attached. He sees us and draws us near. He invites us to follow him and teaches us how to live with freedom from the suffocating effects of unhealthy pressure so that we are liberated into a new reality. His Way moves us beyond our obsessions with self-improvement and the trappings of individualism. It affirms our intrinsic value and our need for one another. It speaks truth to power, confronting authorities and rejecting injustice, while choosing to humbly serve. His Way challenges our greed and invokes our generosity. It dislodges apathy and empowers us to be fruitful. It releases the courage to stand alone and unites us in peace. It enables us to speak hope into hopeless situations; it lifts the burden when we are weighed down, it releases a word of wisdom or knowledge that brings clarity in times of chaos, it heals, delivers and replenishes our depleted souls. It reveals our brokenness to redeem our wholeness. It releases us to love.

When we pattern our lives after Jesus, he promises a new *rhythm*, one that isn't forced. One that doesn't result in us feeling stressed out and anxious, but rather one that is marked by rest, peace and communion with the Father and each other. He exemplifies how this extends beyond our life and into the lives and communities of those around us, but have you ever felt like this message is too good to be true? Have you sometimes sneered at the promise of an 'easy yoke' or tried to *earn* a freedom that is freely given? From our deep-seated drive towards productivity to our struggle to navigate disappointment and loss, how many of us have accepted Jesus but rejected grace? I know I have, but this combination only leads to striving, and it's exhausting.

So how do we distinguish between the pressure that refines and the pressure that causes us to crack? While some pressure is like birth pains producing life, moving us forward to a necessary ending or a desired outcome, other pressure is like dead weight crushing the human spirit, hindering our creativity, robbing our peace and stifling our ability to flourish. When life feels like the equivalent of a pressure cooker, it is suffocation rather than liberation. When the decisions we make are not based on our own convictions but rather the opinions of others, it's a prison. When our identity and our metric for success is patterned on anything other than Christ, we sign up to a game that will always have us on the losing side. It's heavy and burdensome. And yet, the writer of Hebrews exhorts, 'Therefore, since we are surrounded by such a great cloud of witnesses, let us throw off everything that hinders and the sin that so easily entangles. And let us run with perseverance the race marked out for us.'[7]

Pressure Off is a call to throw off the dead weight that conflicts with Christ's message of grace and hinders our ability to love. It's not about shirking responsibility or taking the easy route, it's about choosing the complexity and the grey of a relationship over the simple chequerboard of the law. It's about choosing to step into the light and face the darkness. When our relationships and communities aren't a place where we can be truly authentic, we stop being open. We withdraw, driving our struggles and brokenness under the surface to fester and grow in a condemning silence. When we hide from the Lord, we remove ourselves from the help we need to move forward but when we *come*, he takes the pressure off.

Access All Areas

You may be familiar with the 'triple A pass' used in the entertainment world. AAA stands for 'Access All Areas', meaning you have permission to go anywhere you like at the venue. Similarly, I'd like to highlight some 'triple As' that can really bring life in our discipleship to Jesus: Authenticity, Action and Accountability. These are not steps to success, but rather interconnected values I've found can help us stay open to God.

Authenticity

My goal in this book isn't to tell you what to believe, but rather to encourage you to be honest and bring your whole self before God and the ones you love. To read the Bible and boldly bring your questions to the table in search of understanding. I'm conscious that today 'authentic' has become somewhat of a buzz word and (ironically!) even performative. However, researcher and writer Brené Brown describes 'authenticity' as:

> The daily practice of letting go of who we think we're supposed to be and embracing who we are. Choosing authenticity means cultivating the courage to be imperfect, to set boundaries, and to allow ourselves to be vulnerable; exercising the compassion that comes from knowing that we are all made of strength and struggle; and nurturing the connection and sense of belonging that can only happen when we believe that we are enough.[8]

Choosing authenticity in our world takes courage and it's hard work, but *not* being honest with ourselves is also very hard – just without the joy of connection and sense of belonging at the end of it. If we desire to follow the Way of Jesus, it's important to accept our current location and resist the temptation to fudge things by explaining or spiritualising them away. It is impossible to move forward from where we think we *should be*, only from where we *truly are*. Being in the moment and embracing our story may seem counterintuitive when we are desiring change but it is the very thing that facilitates our transformation.

Action

The philosopher Dallas Willard wrote, 'We don't believe something by merely saying we believe it, or even when we believe that we believe it. We believe something when we act as if it were true.'[9] In the Bible James controversially wrote, faith without works is *dead*.[10] He was not suggesting that we start striving again, but rather that our faith should naturally produce life-giving action. Most significantly, Jesus said, 'Why do you call me, "Lord, Lord," and do not what I say?'[11] Our intentions may be good but, until we yield to God, our faith remains theoretical. For this reason, each chapter is followed by a key spiritual practice that will encourage us to follow the way of Jesus. We often struggle to enact our faith because we have been formed in a world that is in conflict with the kingdom of God. This is why Paul is so emphatic in his appeal for believers to be transformed by the renewing of their minds (with the Greek word for 'transformed' meaning 'proving').[12] This is not just about right belief (orthodoxy) but demonstrable outworking (orthopraxy). The world is patterned and programmed by the prince of the air, Satan (John 12:31) – not the life of grace that is *patterned* after the teachings of Jesus. Romans 12 leads us to active participation with the Scriptures as we experiment, seeking to discern and live out his will. In this sense, spiritual practices can help us to grow in revelation and the grace of God.

Each of the practices shared have community in mind and for good reason. Jesus taught the disciples to pray 'Our Father'; Paul uses 'our Lord' fifty-three times but 'my Lord' only once. As Pastor Rich Villodas also notes, Jesus is never described as 'my' personal saviour in Scripture.[13] The danger of individualism in our Christian living is that it limits the extent of our awareness and collective responsibility beyond self. Action that upholds our interconnectedness orients us towards the kingdom because it reminds us that we belong to each other.

Accountability

Accountability is about the decision to take responsibility for our own actions, recognising perhaps when we've made mistakes and need to make amends or apologise if others are affected. It's also about the choice to invite the feedback of someone we respect and trust, not so that we can blindly follow and do what they say, but so we can grow in wisdom, awareness and maturity. Our main point of accountability is the Lord. Sometimes we can be quick to seek the opinions of others but bringing our situations to God and asking what the gospel has to say first is a healthy discipline that also teaches us discernment.

Accountability can be agreed with anyone from a gym buddy to a spiritual leader or a therapist. To be clear, this is not behaviour policing and nor should it be another source of unhealthy pressure. Rather, it should help us address the things God has highlighted with grace. I am aware that many of us have had painful experiences that may even have closed our hearts to the possibility of Christian community because we have been deeply wounded and I don't encourage us towards accountability lightly. It's important that we feel safe and if there is no one with whom we are ready to engage, choosing to journal our thoughts is another great reflective tool in this area.

Healthy community offers us richness and joy. I have drawn so much strength from sharing and praying with those who have become my closest friends and confidants. Sometimes feedback is challenging, but when given in love, it is also life-giving and empowering. The wounds of a friend are indeed faithful (Proverbs 27:6). Together we are sharpened (Proverbs 27:17), our faith is built up, we are comforted, and we are healed (James 5:16). Within this context, accountability helps us to grow in ways that we cannot on our own.

And finally...

Deep transformation requires us to regularly spend time with God. Sometimes our pride leads us to exhaust all other options but when we humbly recognise our need for him, we pray. Prayer positions us relationally in direct communication with the Lord and empowers us to be effective as believers. To create space to prayerfully process the content of this book, I'll remind you to pause and 'check in' with yourself, individually or in a group, at the end of each chapter. You could read the chapters as a weekly devotional in any order you like. The following questions may be useful in your reflections and prayer time but don't feel like you have to respond to them all. Like the psalmist (Psalms 139:23), ask the Holy Spirit to guide the search within.

Authenticity – What's coming up for me?

- What stood out in this chapter?
- How am I feeling and what do I want?
- What truth am I struggling to live into?
- What's the story I'm telling myself?
- What limitations do I need to accept?

Accountability – What does the gospel say?

- Do I sense God saying anything to me specifically?
- Do I need to ask for help in this area?
- What can I take responsibility for?
- When will I review things?
- Who can I share this with?

Action – What step can I take?

- Do I need to forgive or repent?
- How can I invite the spiritual practice of X into the rhythm of my life?
- What obstacles do I face in doing this and how might I overcome them?
- Do I need to put any healthy boundaries in place?
- How can I yield to God in this area?

Jesus taught the disciples to worship and invite God's will, before petitioning, so this is a good place to start in prayer (Matthew 6:9–13).

As we elevate our adoration above our needs, it reminds us of who God is and lifts our vantage point. Praise asserts God's eternal goodness and is a vital part of our spiritual armour (Ephesians 6:18). We don't have to wait for our circumstances to change before we choose to worship and we are not being insincere when we exalt God in the midst of our mess. Rather it becomes a prophetic statement of our redemptive hope and ignites our faith. Our brains can't respond to anxiety and gratitude simultaneously, so practising thanksgiving also helps to invite calm. Once you've done this, share what's on your heart and boldly come to the throne of our compassionate Lord to ask for the grace you need (Hebrews 4:14–16, 1 Peter 5:7).

In prayer and praise there is a divine exchange. As we look to Jesus and contemplate his glory, our earnest prayers and meditations may at times be all we need to take the pressure off and grab a hold of freedom. At other times it may feel mundane – and that's ok too. Sometimes I've found it more helpful to write my prayers down, to read the prayers of others, sing a song, dance, to sit in silence, shout or just weep. Whatever it looks like, let us accept the invitation to 'Come.'

So, the question remains, at the start of our journey are you willing to give God a triple A pass to your world? To surrender and remove anything that he sees as a hindrance to the healthy rhythm of your life? As you do this, I pray that this book will help you breathe *deeply* and still the waters, so you can address the root of what's troubling them with clarity and truth. May it open your mind and ignite your conversations about what it means to live meaningfully and purposefully in the shadow of the Lord's wonderful grace.

It's time for us to take the pressure off.

1

Pressure off productivity

My nan moved to England from Jamaica in the hope of a better future. Like many of those from the Windrush generation seeking to help reduce Britain's post-war labour shortages, she was greeted with a stony reception. After working in a sewing factory, she began doing sixty-hour weeks in the newly formed NHS to provide for her six children while also taking responsibility for most of the household duties. As a Black woman she often faced unfair treatment in the workplace and subsequently prepared her children for the 'real world' by reminding them that their skin colour meant they needed to work twice as hard as their white counterparts. Now at ninety-two years old, she will often tell me how important it is to do things for yourself; how you can't just depend on others.

My mom was the eldest of her siblings and inherited this same work ethic. She enrolled on degrees, even as a single parent pregnant with her third child, working just as many jobs after she and my dad divorced. With hindsight she now reflects that she didn't *have* to work to the point of burnout, but back then, she didn't know any other way. This was *her* survival and perhaps the fruit of what psychologist and theologian Chanequa Walker-Barnes calls an 'illusion of strength'.[1]

I have huge admiration for both my mother and grandmother; they have endured and overcome hardships and in a lot of ways I am the beneficiary of their sacrifice. However, I am also aware that within me lies the urge to pattern myself after historic acts of survival that don't always lead me into a life marked by grace today. And it turns out, I'm not the only one.

Whether hyper-productivity was modelled in our homes or not, many of us struggle to take our foot off the gas. From stickers in our homework diary at primary school to climbing the career ladder in the workplace, we've been trained to perform our whole lives. And this 'hustle' and 'grind' are often married with unhealthy sleep patterns and an inability to rest, while also being considered the gold standard of work ethic. How many of us find ourselves saying things like, 'I'll sleep when I'm dead' or taking pride in our busy schedules? Meanwhile, beneath the perceived success, accolades and applause, we're struggling to keep our heads above water. Inevitably our capacity changes with different seasons of life but sometimes, not wanting to lose our hard-earned positions, we keep living at the same pace. We fear being forgotten and so continue to post and produce. We try to have and do it all, forgetting or perhaps ignoring the fact that life is seasonal. Our human doing has become so ingrained in the rhythm of our life that we don't know how to stop.

For some, the pressure to have realised your potential by thirty – spouse, house, offspring and car in tow – is overwhelming, and falling behind these externally imposed metrics creates the illusion that we're running out of time. Consciously we know it is unreasonable, but our awareness often fails to halt the current beneath as we strive towards the next best thing. Jesus promises that his 'yoke is easy, and his burden is light' (Matthew 11:30) but can we truly say that we're living in this lightness in the midst of our constant doing? How can we take the pressure off productivity and create lives that flow with the 'unforced rhythms of grace'?

Calling out the counter-productivity

Perhaps the first step is to be honest about the problems caused *by* our so-called 'productivity' – and two areas where I feel the adverse effects of that are in our *work* and in our *world*.

It's so easy to fall into over-productivity in the name of passion. The philosopher Firmin DeBrabander highlighted that there is a 'growing expectation, if not insistence, that work is to be your passion, your obsession – a veritable religion'.[2] He affirms Derek Thompson's article for *The Atlantic* which argues that the 'conception of work has shifted from jobs to careers, to callings'.[3] Coining the term 'workism', Thompson defines it as 'the belief that work is not only necessary to economic production, but also the centerpiece of one's identity and life's purpose'. This is more than simply seeking job satisfaction or trying to make ends meet. Our need for productivity is driving so many of us to find our sense of calling and identity in what we *do*.

When we seek our worthiness in work we may never have that desire quenched – but what if you don't even know what your passions are? A friend shared the stress her ten-year-old daughter felt preparing for the 'dress up as who you want to be when you're older' day in primary school. We often feel the pressure to possess some great sense of purpose from an early age, but while the path may emerge quickly for some, for the majority of us, our passions are more of a discovery process. So why do we try to force it? And while it's a joy to do the work that we love, equally, not every passion requires a route to market, nor do we need to squeeze every inch of productivity out of it. Sometimes it seems like we can't have a passion – whether singing, reading, painting or gardening – without turning it into *work*. Maybe the lessons born of adversity can provide some wisdom to help disentangle us.

Like my grandmother, having worked under oppressive circumstances while trying to retain the economic power of a pay cheque, the late Toni Morrison concluded, 'You are not the work you do; you are the person you are.'[4] Her experience taught her that measuring our life by the level of our work is a disordered way of being. Morrison's own path spanned from teaching, to becoming a mother, to working as an editor in publishing houses, to writing novels, plays and even texts for classical music. Passions and careers may change but the value of who we are remains constant.

Our neglect of the world around us is another painful reminder of our hyper-productivity and it affects the vulnerable most acutely. Climate change, for example, is 'predominantly caused by the richest countries and mainly suffered by the poorest', who also have the toxic waste of the wealthy dumped on them.[5] Alerted to the unsustainable ways in which we have been living, there has been a surge in new conversations about how we can better take care of the planet we inhabit. In retail, many of my friends are turning to sites like Vinted and eco-friendly brands for their shopping needs. But when it comes to going green day-to-day, according to a recent article in the *Harvard Business Review*, there's a significant need for us to narrow what has been called the 'intention–action gap'.[6] It's time to let our good intentions shape our actions:

> Unilever, estimates that almost 70% of its greenhouse gas footprint depends on which products customers choose and whether they use and dispose of them in a sustainable manner – for example, by conserving water and energy while doing the laundry or recycling containers properly after use.[7]

In the age of convenience, our push for productivity often ends up being counterproductive and peeling away the layers can feel like an impossible task. For Canadian writer and social activist Naomi Klein, a whole new ethos is required:

> While it is true that climate change is a crisis produced by an excess of greenhouse gases in the atmosphere, it is also, in a more profound sense, a crisis produced by an extractive mind-set, by a way of viewing both the natural world and the majority of its inhabitants as resources to use up and then

discard. I call it the 'gig and dig' economy and firmly believe that we will not emerge from this crisis without a shift in worldview at every level, a transformation to an ethos of care and repair. Repairing the land. Repairing our stuff. Fearlessly repairing our relationships within our countries and between them.[8]

Through the challenges, there are signs that we are beginning to re-evaluate the metrics of our success in ways that have the potential to reform our connection with each other and the environment. We *want* to slow down our productivity and we're setting our intentions but how do we resist the temptation to fall back into old habits? How might the way of Jesus speak to our need for both productivity and connection in a busy world?

Already approved?

While we spend our whole lives being praised and rewarded for our performance, the Bible reveals the Father's great pleasure in Jesus *before* his ministry began. Immediately after being baptised by John, it is recorded 'And a voice from heaven said, "This is my Son, whom I love; with him I am well pleased"' (Matthew 3:17). Sometimes we are caught up in performing to the point of burnout because we are seeking approval, yet Jesus was aware of his Father's pleasure before he had performed a single miracle or preached to the masses. This moment, I believe, points us to a key truth about God's grace: we can't earn it. The gift of salvation is just that – a *gift*. Paul's letter to the church in Ephesus reminds us that we are not saved because of our good deeds and productivity, but rather our good deeds are a consequence of the Lord making us new: 'For it is by grace you have been saved, through faith – and this is not from yourselves, it is the gift of God – not by works, so that no one can boast' (Ephesians 2:8–9).

With this foundational truth in mind, our church communities should be free of this approval-driven productivity, right? And yet, in reality, society's celebration of an individual's ability to demonstrate high capacity more than their ability to rest is mirrored in our congregations too. In the midst of all the sermons encouraging us toward bigger, greater and better things, we push ourselves beyond healthy boundaries in the name of the Lord. Typically 20% of the people – mostly women – burn out doing 80% of the labour, leaving both staff and volunteers overworked and under-resourced in many of our communities. In her book, *Celebrities for Jesus*, writer Katelyn Beaty states that:

> Of course, sacrifice and devotion are part and parcel of the Christian life … it's not always clear whether members are being called to sacrifice for Christ or for the church and its programs. Loyalty to Christ and loyalty to the founding pastor's vision can get muddled.[9]

Speaking with a friend about her time serving on a church internship, she recalls being questioned about her need for a day off when already volunteering five days a week on top of a part-time job that paid her bills. Although there was a clear willingness to serve, those struggling with the demand were encouraged to ask God to give them a *bigger plate*, not to slow down. Sometimes the pressure on productivity is not in the name of the Lord at all but rather a result of systemic issues and abuses of power. For some of us, our Christian experience has glorified suffering and not taught us the difference between healthy and positive self-denial. In turn, we may fear that slowing down will signal a lack of faith or disappoint those who need us so we shoulder the burden and succumb to the pressure of a weight we weren't intended to carry. We remain in situations that are inflicting wounds on our souls and even our bodies when the path of grace is leading us towards freedom.

Releasing ourselves to be honest about the impact of what we are going through can help us to define our experience. Is this making me unwell? Is there an end in sight? Even Jesus pleaded in Gethsemane for the cup of death to be taken away from him and he did not suffer an endless crucifixion. His example empowers us to endure suffering but it also empowers us to articulate our pain and challenge harmful situations, to enquire of the Lord and seek understanding with the ultimate desire to do his will.

Pressure to perform was a problem for the early church too and often featured in letters to the Gentiles who were being coaxed by the Judaisers to be circumcised according to the law in order to attain righteousness. Galatians 3:1–3 reveals Paul's frustrations:

> You foolish Galatians! Who has bewitched you? Before your very eyes Jesus Christ was clearly portrayed as crucified. I would like to learn just one thing from you: did you receive the Spirit by the works of the law, or by believing what you heard? Are you so foolish? After beginning by means of the Spirit, are you now trying to finish by means of the flesh?

Paul understood that without grace, the Christian life would be impossible. The law never produced the kind of fruit that God desired. The law produced an outward show and religious performance without transformation of the heart. Exhaustion, cynicism and apathy can be signs that we are trying to sustain our lives without the enabling power and guidance of the Holy Spirit. Being judgemental towards others or enduring feelings of guilt, jealousy and shame are some of the indicators that we are defining ourselves with a performance-based mindset.

Grasping the concept of God's grace in a competitive world is tough. Resisting the temptation to not live for human applause and be overly concerned with what people think about us is a challenge. Understanding that the value of our life is credited to God, not to our own ability or inability to perform well, is humbling and countercultural. In his kingdom we serve and live *from* acceptance rather than *to* acceptance. The value God places on us is reflected in our being created in his image and also in his willingness to sacrifice his life as a ransom for ours while we were still sinners (Romans 5:8). If we remain connected and committed to honesty, we will be aware of whether our activities are born of our insecurity or our completeness in him. This liberates us to serve from a place of gratitude and grace. The end result may look the same, but the process by which we get there is very different, and we know it. In this place our self-esteem is kept intact and the peace of God is ours. Knowing and believing that we are pleasing to God before we do a single thing is a game changer.

The connected life

Most of us who have been following Jesus for some time will know that we are already approved in theory, but sometimes struggle to live this truth out in practice. So how do we prevent ourselves from forgetting God's grace as we try to adopt a healthy approach to productivity?

This question was brought to the fore as I sat in a church service shortly after my family and I moved from Birmingham to Manchester. As the preacher shared a sermon on John 15, God reminded me powerfully through a familiar story that Jesus is the life-source and that my ability to be fruitful is dependent only on my connectedness to him.

I am the true vine, and my Father is the gardener. He cuts off every branch in me that bears no fruit, while every branch that does bear fruit, he prunes so that it will be even more fruitful. You are already clean because of the word I have spoken to you. *Remain* in me, as I also *remain* in you. No

21

branch can bear fruit by itself; it must *remain* in the vine. Neither can you bear fruit unless you *remain* in me.

I am the vine; you are the branches. If you *remain* in me and I in you, you will bear much fruit; apart from me you can do nothing. If you do not *remain* in me, you are like a branch that is thrown away and withers; such branches are picked up, thrown into the fire and burned. If you *remain* in me and my words *remain* in you, ask whatever you wish, and it will be done for you. This is to my Father's glory, that you bear much fruit, showing yourselves to be my disciples.
(John 15:1–9, emphasis mine)

As I listened, I became aware that my sense of worth had indeed become tied to what I do. I was so desperate to be fruitful and do something significant in my life, but through this message he showed me how I'd been leaving him out of the journey. He was my first true love but, in this moment, I realised how he had subtly slipped out of focus. Other desires outside of him had crept in along with my insecurities and he was no longer the goal in the way he had been at the start.

Jesus repeatedly asks us to 'remain' in him, I believe, because he knows our propensity to stray. We may start with him, but he is teaching us to *continue* with him also. I tried with all my might, but fulfilment would never be attained in the strength of my five and ten year plans. Fulfilment wouldn't be found in my ability to do, it was in my ability to *be*. I cried involuntarily, tears of repentance. Spirit to spirit. My head would catch up later, but this moment was a divine exchange. Healing grace to start all over again, like the first time when he rescued my soul.

It was in the following months of prioritising time with the Lord amid the busyness of life that I truly began to understand the grace of God beyond a simple definition. It's so easy to fall into the rat race, and become disconnected from Jesus, even from our own hearts. However, when we abide, we are more likely to hear clearly, we are sensitive to his direction and to his tugs. We receive grace, we are renewed and refreshed, and we pray prayers that are inspired by heaven.

Connected to self

Through prioritising my connection with God, I became more connected with myself, focusing less on what I was *doing* and more on who I was *becoming*.

Oftentimes, our productivity is directed by a vision to see a particular outcome. It could be eradicating homelessness, providing for our family, getting a first-class degree or becoming a world leader. Each one of these ambitions has merit but more than our drive for world peace, Jesus wants our hearts. If we are providing food for the poor across the world but oppressing our neighbours, which one of these actions most reveals the condition of our hearts? If we are preaching up a storm but abusing our spouse, how will God respond to our duplicity? Jesus taught his disciples:

> Not everyone who says to me, 'Lord, Lord,' will enter the kingdom of heaven, but only the one who does the will of my Father who is in heaven. Many will say to me on that day, 'Lord, Lord, did we not prophesy in your name and in your name drive out demons and in your name perform many miracles?' Then I will tell them plainly, 'I never knew you. Away from me, you evildoers!'
> (Matthew 7:21–23)

It is possible to do great things, even in the name of the Lord, and yet find ourselves far from him. It is clear that Jesus is more concerned with who we are becoming than what we achieve or what we do. David Wilkerson, pastor and author of *The Cross and the Switchblade*, contended that:

> If I am not Christ-like at heart – if I'm not becoming notice-ably more like him – I have totally missed God's purpose for my life. It doesn't matter what I accomplish for his kingdom. If I miss this one purpose, I have lived, preached and striven in vain ... You see, God's purpose for me can't be fulfilled by what I do for Christ. It can't be measured by anything I achieve, even if I heal the sick or cast out demons. No, God's purpose is fulfilled in me only by what I am becoming in him. Christlikeness isn't about what I do for the Lord, but about how I'm being transformed into his likeness.[10]

Far from being defined by his performance, Jesus modelled a way of life that was countercultural and, in becoming like him, our view of productivity and the way we choose to live our lives may look different to our culture too.

I was typing away in my local coffee shop one morning, shoulder jigging, singing along to the background music when I looked up from my work to see that the lady sat on the opposite table to me had caught me dancing. We both laughed and soon got talking. Her name was Kerry and she was thirty-four. She said that she worked in a fast-paced, performance-driven environment but had recently reduced her working hours to four days a week to improve her work–life balance. She had just completed a skydive that morning on her day off. Kerry shared that some of her colleagues couldn't understand why she would reduce her earning potential, but she explained that even though she was earning less money than ever, she was also less stressed and happier than she'd ever been. The deci-sion to prioritise her *becoming* over producing was more important.

Sometimes, as Christians, we can hear stories like this and yet still feel that the Lord is calling us to do more and achieve more with our God-given time. But maybe what our gracious God is asking of us is really kind. Letting go of a role, choosing a smaller pay packet or saying 'no' has the ability to release us into a greater level of freedom and presence in a world where it never quite feels like we're doing enough. It may not look like we are progressing outwardly but there is healthy and enduring growth taking place beneath the dermis. Sometimes we're learning contentment and the value of simple habits in the rhythm of life.

In her 1988 essay collection, *A Burst of Light*, writer and activist Audre Lorde famously said, 'Caring for myself is not self-indulgence, it is self-preservation, and that is an act of political warfare.'[11] In 2023, her words echo in the lives of Black women who have chosen to reject the strong Black woman trope in exchange for a 'soft life', a movement that places emphasis on self-care. Their rationale is one I resonate with deeply and it should be noted that self-care doesn't need to be selfish, nor does it have to be an expensive luxury. Our diet and exercise are also other significant markers of wellbeing. It's important to recognise the contradictory ways in which large corporations commercialise our need for self-care so that we don't fall prey to their high-pressure marketing. When we centre our wellbeing on luxury, we risk undoing our progress because our care remains dependent on our production – and the cycle of pressure continues.

Connected to others

Remaining in the vine helps us remain connected to God and connected to ourselves in a way that truly takes the pressure off productivity, but the Lord also designed us to remain connected to one another. He commands us to love our neighbours as ourselves.

Collectively, the Bible refers to believers as the body of Christ, representing the way in which we are intended to fit together. Our productivity is intended to be the result of both a connected and collective output. Each part or person has been purposefully placed as God intended and their significance is not determined by human standards. Those that one would expect to be of lesser regard because of their function, are actually given greater honour by the Lord so that each part has equal concern for the other.

> But in fact God has placed the parts in the body, every one of them, just as he wanted them to be. If they were all one part, where would the body be? As it is, there are many parts, but one body. The eye cannot say to the hand, 'I don't need you!' And the head cannot say to the feet, 'I don't need you!' On the contrary, those parts of the body that seem to be weaker are indispensable, and the parts that we think are less honourable we treat with special honour. And the parts that are unpresentable are treated with special modesty, while our presentable parts need no special treatment. But God has put the body together, giving greater honour to the parts that lacked it, so that there should be no division in the body, but that its parts should have equal concern for each other. If one part suffers, every part suffers with it; if one part is honoured, every part rejoices with it.
> (1 Corinthians 12:18–26)

What a powerful picture of unity – a picture that challenges the competitive and everyone-for-themselves mentality which dominates our working world today (not to mention, the devaluing of essential workers who uphold our society, often for the least reward). Trying to do life alone is a source of pressure because we need each other to function. By humbly honouring the equal value of each person, the Bible teaches that we all benefit.

Succumbing to the pressure to produce means we are more likely to compromise our values and calling – but the responsibility of stewardship and an awareness of our collective responsibility challenge our passivity. When the drive for 'success' has us tread-milling through life like a hamster on a wheel, it's revolutionary to stand still.

Key spiritual practice: Rest

Sunday shop closures ended in the early 1990s, but the call for Sabbath rest hasn't changed. Jesus often pulled himself away from the crowds to be alone in silence with the Father and the Lord still commands us to rest, just as he did following the work he carried out in creation.

> Remember the Sabbath day by keeping it holy. Six days you shall labour and do all your work, but the seventh day is a sabbath to the LORD your God. On it you shall not do any work, neither you, nor your son or daughter, nor your male or female servant, nor your animals, nor any foreigner residing in your towns. For in six days the LORD made the heavens and the earth, the sea, and all that is in them, but he rested on the seventh day. Therefore, the LORD blessed the Sabbath day and made it holy.
> (Exodus 20:8–11)

After delivering the Israelites from Egypt, the Lord commanded them to keep the Sabbath. Under Egyptian rule, they worked constantly without rest under harsh conditions, but now in their freedom, God was telling them to stop. This was countercultural for them, and it rewrote history.

Today, the Sabbath continues to tell us the story of who we are: that we are no longer slaves and we are not defined by how much work we do. It is an act of liberation, as we rest, to honour the image of our heavenly Father in us and sense his pleasure. His approval, his choosing and his love. Sabbath creates room to let go of external pressures from society, family and worldly ideas of success as we are reminded that we are free to be who God has created us to be. As author Pete Scazzero once tweeted: 'The limit of Sabbath keeps us grounded and humble reminding us that we are not in charge of running the world. It breaks our self-will and grows us in wisdom.'[12] In this sense, Sabbath rest is also an act of trust and a reminder that it is God who holds the universe together. In our rest we are reminded that we are sustained only by his Spirit. We create room for the miraculous, room to rethink our challenges and fears with the mind of Christ.

It was in love that God commanded the Sabbath but, as we have seen, a culture of hyper-productivity will have us believing that rest is a luxury we can't afford. We must recognise the things in our life that uphold this narrative so that we can challenge them and form new habits. For example, a friend of mine committed to setting her phone screen to the black-and-white mode to reduce the desire to reach for it constantly, and she turns it off completely every Friday. Her decision to hit pause and do nothing is part of her commitment to following the way of Jesus, and its results are tangible. They may not be the type of results that the world celebrates – but they're results that help her 'soul catch up with her body' so she can live into grace.[13]

The movie *Chariots of Fire*[14] was inspired by the story of British runner, Eric Liddell. Liddell was the favourite to win the 100 metres for the British Olympic Team in the 1924 Paris Olympic Games but when it was announced that the heats would fall on a Sunday, his chosen day of worship and rest, Liddell refused to compete and was forced to withdraw from his best event. For Liddell, the glory of God was more important than the glory of man. Although his competitor took home the 100 metres, he chose to compete in the 400-metre race and unexpectedly took away a gold medal along with an Olympic world record. Resisting the drive of productivity as a professional athlete, he is famously quoted as saying: 'I believe

God made me for a purpose, but he also made me fast. And when I run, I feel His pleasure.'

When our abilities and accomplishments become a means of evidencing our sense of value, it creates a work-based mindset and a barrier to our reception of the grace of God. The Sabbath reminds us that our life is not a performance, it is an outward expression of an inward transformation. The show is over because the most outstanding performance has already been delivered through the cross by our most excellent Saviour. He wants us to be productive – not from a place of pressure, but from a place of rest, sensing his pleasure as we work. And that truly takes the pressure off.

Let's take a pause and 'check in'. Look back at page 12 for some questions to help you reflect.

2

Pressure off perfection

Song writing is a wellspring for me – one that perfectionism has the power to stem the flow of. But when I *don't* allow perfectionism to grind my creativity to a halt, the most precious moments happen. I'm less inhibited, less self-conscious and more accepting of myself. I am liberated to explore the corridors of my creativity without fear; I'm more guttural, more instinctive, and I don't worry about dead ends. It requires me to not judge the process too soon but enjoy the exploration of sounds, chords and harmony until something sticks. Sometimes I'm amazed at what surfaces in these times when I'm relaxed and at ease. I've written many songs that have come to nothing, but I love the freedom of the process; it has a healing quality, it's my happy place and it's where I'm content.

When perfectionism is present, it's a different story. Perfectionism has us warding off impending doom in such a way that it robs us of the possibilities and the joy of the present. During my younger years, more often than not, I would feel awful after a performance. One mistake would overshadow the whole and there were times when I'd even struggle to sleep at night going over everything that fell short of my high standards. In those moments I felt like a failure but, as we know, it's what we do with our *experiences* of failure that matters. To create something new out of nothing and to grow in any discipline requires trial and error. So why does perfectionism have such a hold on us?

Aesthetics

It's hard to imagine a world without social media. It's been an invaluable tool for me in releasing music and, especially after moving cities, I've really appreciated being able to share life updates with family and friends. And yet, it's definitely consumed far too much of my time. Furthermore, once the Instagram grid appeared, it wasn't just about sharing, it was about aesthetics. We exist in an imperfect world, filled with imperfect people yet more than ever, we're striving for 'show home' lives and we're *tired*.

The boom in the medical cosmetic and beauty industry reflects our global obsession with body perfection. There's always something more to tweak and we're never quite satisfied. We have photoshopped, filtered and contoured beyond recognition and it's leaving our self-worth in tatters. Author and researcher, Brené Brown says that:

> Perfectionism is a self destructive and addictive belief system that fuels this primary thought: If I look perfect, and do everything perfectly, I can avoid or minimize the painful feelings of shame, judgement, and blame. … Healthy striving is self-focused: 'How can I improve?' Perfectionism is other-focused: 'What will they think?'[1]

While we all agree it's important to look after our 'temples', behind our seemingly harmless attention to beauty, health and fitness lie many hidden struggles with body image. Big brands like Dove and celebrities such as Alicia Keys are trying to buck the beauty trend in promoting body positivity for women, and men are also challenging the prevailing narrative. Actor Justin Baldoni spoke about his struggle with body dysmorphia in a TED talk detailing the pressure he experienced doing shirtless filming, while actor John Boyega has spoken up saying he wants to create movies that reflect a diversity of body types because, he challenges, 'Why do leads always have to be muscular and ripped?'[2] Speaking to Hypebeast, he also said, 'It's about rebranding the way in which we are fed a false narrative of perfection.' These conversations are particularly heartening to me, as a mother of three boys who are in the modelling field, but it's hard to ignore the fact that 'perceived perfection' is an increasing trend with harmful outcomes.

Psychologists Thomas Curran and Andrew P. Hill produced a study into perfectionism, categorising it across three main descriptors: self-oriented perfectionism, other-oriented perfectionism and socially prescribed perfectionism.[3] Of the three, socially prescribed perfectionism (in other words, perceived external societal pressures) was described as the 'most debilitating' due to its serious impact on our mental health and its contribution to rising rates of depression and anxiety. Besides beauty standards, so many of us struggle with perfectionism-related pressure that manifests as fear of failure, over-achieving, catastrophising, people-pleasing and struggling to celebrate success to name a few. If productivity says *do* more, perfectionism says *be* more. If productivity says you aren't *doing* enough, perfectionism says *you aren't enough*. Speaking in an interview, Curran stated,

> Perfectionism at root is a need and a requirement to be perfect, because ultimately, we feel that we're flawed, that we're defective and that there's something imperfect about us that needs to be repaired. And it's that deficit thinking that really drives perfectionism.[4]

It reflects a deep sense of unworthiness that seeks to remedy the lack of value we feel internally, with external outcomes.

Positively, Gen Z are definitely trying to change this narrative and it's reflected in things like their platform shift from the likes of the perfect grids of Instagram to BeReal and TikTok, which brands itself as a 'home for authentic expression and integrity'. However, the statistics reveal that the problem is growing at a faster rate than their efforts to curb what is a complex issue. Social media, advertising, increased competition in education and parental expectations are some of the reasons Curran cites to explain why the belief that we need to be perfect is increasing, especially among young people. 'They're all drawn together by a move and a shift in broader culture towards a market society, which has emphasis on things like competition, meritocracy, hard work.'[5] Specifically commenting on social media pressure, he says that this 'deficit thinking' is being fuelled by economic agendas that profit off the misery of the next generation because 'if you can punch holes in people's lives, they'll purchase things to try to fill them'.

When profit is involved, we can't rely on brands to lead us towards liberation. But what about the church – a place where we invite people to come as they are, can they really do that?

Messy Church

Churches are messy places because they are full of complex people with different (and sometimes difficult) backgrounds and stories. Any attempt to sanitise ourselves or others because they don't fit into our neatly packaged boxes creates pressure and it inhibits a true sense of belonging. Sadly, however, like wider society, churches are also breeding grounds for a struggle with perfectionism and can have us 'keeping up appearances' on a weekly basis. False expectations about what it means to be a godly man or woman can weigh heavily and we don't always know how to dismantle them.

Livestreaming has also added another layer of perfection pressure to our church communities. The pandemic forced many of us online for the first time and now many congregations are kitted out with some sort of lighting, camera, flat screen and sound system to facilitate the global transmission of their services. Being able to connect in this way has blessed people and helped to facilitate the preaching of the gospel to great effect. However, the line between excellence and perfectionism can get blurred sometimes and it is this proximity to excellence and on-the-surface positive outcomes that makes perfectionism so hard to detect and challenge. There are no issues with digital media tools in and of themselves, it's the culture they can create when not kept in their rightful place. The attention required to facilitate them can detract from our ability to have the genuine human connection our world is craving.

When our services become intricately crafted and timed encounters, we lose authenticity, freedom and true worship. Furthermore, we subsequently disciple our congregation into the shallowness of our expression. Many worship leaders lead in fear of putting a foot wrong, not because of a lack of spiritual maturity, gift or passion but because of the pressure to put on a faultless delivery. An over-emphasis on slick presentation makes worship a revered spectator sport and the platform the goal, whereas an emphasis on genuine and liberated expression results in encounter and a hunger for God. Perfectionism in the church and the culture is disheartening and overwhelming at times, but what hope might we find in Jesus to cut through the barrage both out there and within?

The 'already not yet'

It is easy to be drawn into false ideals that suggest being a Christian equates to a perfect life but the truth is that we live in the 'already not yet'. Although we believe that eternity has already begun, we have not yet received all that Christ has in store for us. We are saved and eternity *has* begun – but we understand that we will experience pain in this life and that our bodies will pass away. We are already redeemed and have a spiritual inheritance that we are receiving now – but there is more to receive when Christ returns. We are citizens of heaven dwelling on the earth and we experience the paradox of trying to live with a dual residency that requires us not to be too heavenly-minded, but not totally defined by our humanity either.

One of the reasons why I lacked confidence as an artist is because I constantly berated myself in relation to other artists I admired. While it is great to be inspired, choosing to 'follow' other people whom we think are a success shouldn't come at the cost of accepting ourselves for who we are. If in attempting perfection we are trying to be someone else and comparing ourselves with others, the Bible teaches that we are being unwise. In a world that has us constantly sizing ourselves up to superficial and changeable standards, our struggle for perfectionism is not just external, sometimes we are our own worst enemy. In order to tackle perfectionism we need truths that are able to endure and hold us beyond the fragility and inconsistencies of our human nature. A set of values that establish our worth on the mountaintop, in the valley and everywhere in between. I believe that the challenge is to develop a healthy understanding and acceptance of ourselves in the light of our new identity and position in Christ.

A Christ-centred self-concept

Attending therapy has been one of the most significant steps towards self-acceptance for me. In therapeutic thought the self-concept refers to how we think about, evaluate and perceive ourselves and answers the question: *who am I?* It is influenced by our upbringing, relationships and life experiences and is made up of our self-image, self-esteem and ideal self. Our 'true self', although constantly evolving, is who we really are. Often we feel the pressure of the expectations from our many influences. Trying to filter through them to discern what we think for ourselves or what we believe God's will is can be difficult. Sometimes we don't have the confidence to do it. This is not a zero-sum exchange though. Living out the convictions and expectations of other people instead of our own creates an internal dissonance. Our true self is in a perpetual state of playing catch up and feeling like we are never quite good enough. We feel like a fraud because we struggle to live authentically. When our internal world is incongruent with our external reality, it creates pressure. From this place it's hard to have the honest conversations and prayers that help move us forward.

While we may be unable to fully disentangle ourselves from the influences we have received from infancy, the Bible tells us that when we receive Jesus into our heart, we are born again and given a fresh start. When we truly follow him, like a parent to a child, he becomes the dominant influence on our life and teaches us how to live well. In this sense, our self-concept becomes Christ-centred. He informs every area of our lives as we seek to apply the lens of the gospel to our experiences now that we have become new: 'Therefore, if anyone is in Christ, the new creation has come: The old has gone, the new is here!' (2 Corinthians 5:17). This is the ongoing process of sanctification. If you have accepted Jesus, put your faith in what he did on the cross and invited him to be Lord of your life, your identity first and foremost is a Child of God. 'Yet to all who did receive him, to those who believed in his name, he gave the right to become children of God' (John 1:12). God created every single person on this planet to reflect his glory and be an image bearer. As we discover more of who he is, we discover more of who we are. Whatever we have been through and whatever has happened to us cannot undermine our intrinsic value. When we grab a hold of this truth, it helps to remove us from both the internal and external pressures of perfectionism because the value that has been ascribed to us affirms our sufficiency in Christ and rejects the deficiency mindset that is perpetuated in society.

We are all full of imperfections. There is always going to be something that we could be better at, improve upon or be more knowledgeable in and this is also what makes us human. The pressures of living with our humanity and also our spiritual reality must be truly heard if we are to be liberated but as Christians our spiritual identity must lead the conversation. The theologian John Piper said:

Christian selfhood is not defined in terms of who we are in and of ourselves. It's defined in terms of what God does to us and the relationship he creates with us and the destiny he appoints for us. In other words as a Christian you cannot talk about your identity without talking about the action of God on you, the relationship of God with you, and the purpose of God for you. The biblical understanding of human self-identity is radically God-centred.[6]

Despite our tendency to move away from fragility, the unconditional love of God creates an environment for self-acceptance and vulnerability. Knowing that we are sons and daughters, worthy and secure in Christ helps us to accept our weaknesses and renders the accusations of perfectionism powerless. This releases us again to experience the grace of our God, who chooses to use us in spite of our flaws.

This is captured beautifully for me by the Japanese art of Kintsugi that repairs broken ceramics with gold or silver. The repaired work, having been broken, is considered to be more beautiful than its previous state. If we imagine that the cracks in Kintsugi are symbolic of our imperfections, then the gold is symbolic of the Lord's glory. It represents the work of his grace, his healing, his redemption, his power in putting us back together and allowing us to have purpose again.

Jars of clay

The Apostle Paul, writing to the church in Corinth – who had previously rejected him because his life looked less 'perfect' than other more wealthy and eloquent Christian leaders – said: 'We have this treasure in jars of clay that the excellency will be of God and not of us' (2 Corinthians 4:7). There is freedom for us all in the truth that God has chosen to put his precious Spirit in our *fragile* clay pots. What a humbling privilege it is to serve the Lord! Like the art of Kintsugi, we are *more* beautiful because of the Lord's redemptive work. Not because we've got it all together, but because, by his grace, he holds us together. When grace gives us the ability to reconcile with a loved one, it reveals the glory of God. If we pretend that we're not hurt, we're covering the cracks. The glory is revealed in our authenticity as well as our availability. In our humanity as well as our heavenwardness. God knows our weaknesses and loves us in spite of them all. He lived a perfect life and died a criminal's death to atone for them, because of his great love. This is why salvation is the most powerful revelation of his glory. It doesn't erase our story, it beautifies it. Jesus has shown us how to live, not so that we can be in a continual state of discontentment as we strive for perfection, but so that we are continually aware of our dependence on him. Our pride pulls us away from this truth and leads us into striving and comparison, but humility draws us towards a healthy acceptance of our weakness and grace.

But what about accepting the limitations of others? We relate to people most significantly when we keep it real but what if experiencing someone else's vulnerability makes us feel uncomfortable? In her book, *My Body Is Not a Prayer Request*, Amy Kenny reflects on one of many encounters with a stranger offering to pray for her disability:

> She simply interprets my cane as something that requires 'fixing' and ropes God into her ableism, the belief that disabled people are less valuable or less human than our nondisabled counterparts... To assume that my disability needs to be erased in order for me to live an abundant life is disturbing not only because of what it says about me but also because of what it reveals about people's notions of God. I bear the image of the Alpha and the Omega. My disabled body is a temple for the Holy Spirit. I have the mind of Christ. There's no caveat to those promises. I don't have a junior Holy Spirit because I am disabled. To suggest that I am anything less than sanctified and redeemed is to suppress the image of God in my disabled body and to limit how God is already at work through my life.[7]

I found Amy's story incredibly moving and brave. As Christians we often think that God's power will be seen most significantly if we pray away all those things we consider to be weak. Not taking this stance can be uncomfortable because it challenges our perception of how God operates in the world. My friend Fiona Godsden has a lifelong rare bone disorder that significantly affects her energy and mobility. She shared that while it's hard to come to terms with the restrictions that disability brings at times, choosing to accept our limitations is important. Contrary to how we may feel, Fiona encouraged that, 'Limitations are something we can celebrate, they're not something to be ashamed of.'[8] Similarly, stigmas around poor mental health can leave people feeling deficient or lacking faith when their condition persists. Some of us will need medical intervention and therapeutic care *as well as* prayer to function – and that's ok.

Speaking about an area of personal weakness that he asked the Lord to remove, Paul writes, 'But he said to me, "My grace is sufficient for you, for my power is made perfect in weakness." Therefore, I will boast all the more gladly about my weaknesses, so that Christ's power may rest on me' (2 Corinthians 12:9). This truth challenges how we talk about weakness, especially on behalf of others. Over the past eight years, I've been so inspired by the life and work of another friend, Emma Pinnock, who specialises in SEND support for families and schools. Through our conversations she has shared the importance of confronting stigmas and language around neurodiversity that see it as a problem to be fixed. Her encouragement to 'uniquely take your place' in a perfection-driven world that 'others' those of us with needs is prophetic.

Embracing the 'perceived imperfections' among us and having a Christ-centred self-concept reveals our fragility and it also reveals a more holistic picture of redemption. It releases us all to recognise that it's not our job to be perfect, but to point to the one who is.

Key spiritual practice: Worship

In 2011, I left my teaching job to work part-time with women in prison and on probation. Over the following two years I had a steep learning curve into the heart-breaking realities of life for many women as I facilitated sessions on relationships, confidence-building, self-esteem, abuse, sexual health, mental health and employability. There was such an honesty and rawness about these times, and I saw how beautiful, precious and resilient these women were. I also began to learn in practice how empowering it truly is when we allow ourselves to be seen. Leaving prison one afternoon I heard the sound of singing but I couldn't work out where it was coming from. As I traced the voices, it led me to the chapel where a group of women were singing their hearts out. I was so moved that in the months that followed I visited the chapel on a Sunday to join the service. The atmosphere was electric, and these occasions I remember to this day as some of the most beautiful worship moments I've ever had. Through my sessions with some of the most vulnerable and scorned women in society I experienced how liberating it is for ourselves and others when we let go of perfection and change our 'normal' to something that is far more genuine and real. Through these same women I also witnessed a reckless abandonment in worship.

In the book of Exodus, after delivering the Israelites from Egypt, the Lord establishes specific rituals, roles and instruments for them to use in worship, and provides the Ten Commandments to guide them on how to live. At the physical centre of the community, in the Holy of Holies, was the ark of the covenant. This was where God's manifest presence could be found and only the high priest could enter once a year to offer sacrifices. Israel's worship and the law established them as God's people, distinct from the nations around them. By establishing worship through animal sacrifices for the forgiveness of sins, the Lord made it possible for them to be near – and notably, when the people brought their offerings, the priest wasn't looking to see how repentant the person was or at the magnitude of the sin. What was important was the quality of the sacrifice. The animal had to be perfect, not crippled or diseased but the best they could find.

Jesus' appearance in human history is recorded in the New Testament but his entry into our world was a fulfilment of everything that was written about him and prophesied thousands of years prior. The law along with the worship practices recorded in the Old Testament were only a shadow of a reality that was revealed in Christ – they set us up for the unblemished Lamb of God. Just as the priests lay their hands on the animal being sacrificed and confessed the sins of the people, the sins of the entire world were appropriated to Jesus on the cross. There is no condemnation for those who are in Christ, because God looks at us through his *perfect* sacrifice and deems us righteous.

As a worship leader, one of the most challenging things is to lay aside my own self-consciousness, without leaving my person behind. To acknowledge the people before me authentically but to have a God-consciousness that supersedes any evaluations of my capabilities or desire to be applauded. This is also the journey I seek to take the congregation on. To encourage them to bring their whole selves into an intentional and authentic moment, void of the self-consciousness that obstructs our connection. As theologian C. S. Lewis wrote, 'The real test of being in the presence of God is that you either forget about yourself altogether or you see yourself as a small, dirty object. It is better to forget about yourself altogether.'[9] In worship we have the opportunity to take the focus off ourselves and put it on God in a radical way. To become more God-conscious than self-conscious in a selfie-driven world.

When our worship becomes a lifestyle, it changes the atmosphere of our life. Like those that brought their sacrifices, the Lord invites us to come boldly and present ourselves. As we do, he embeds his truth in our hearts in such a way that it reorients the way we think about others and ourselves. In his book, *The Freedom of Self-forgetfulness*, Tim Keller writes, 'Like Paul, we can say, "I don't care what you think. I don't even care what I think. I only care about what the Lord thinks."'[10] A culture that teaches us to erase imperfections feeds the lie that God cannot use us until we earn our way to righteousness. It conflicts with Christ's message of grace and acceptance and undermines our position as children of God. It is a barrier to the truth that his strength is perfected in our weakness and that the acceptance of our fragility is a humbling reminder of how glorious he is! It is a stumbling block because our vulnerability is a doorway to our reception of him and perfectionism leaves us disillusioned when life doesn't go to plan. It even leads us to reject and dehumanise each other.

However, when we bring our strength *and* weaknesses into God's presence and truly exalt him above ourselves in worship, it transforms our perspective and we use the right yardsticks to measure success. The forgetfulness we experience diffuses into our everyday lives and when perfectionism comes knocking, in humility we find the grace to submit the deficiency of our human standards to the supernatural sufficiency of the cross. Pressure *off*.

Let's take a pause and 'check in'. Look back at page 12 for some questions to help you reflect.

3

Pressure off singleness

Believe it or not, I wasn't that young girl flicking through wedding magazines dreaming of the day when it would be my turn to walk down the aisle. My parents separated when I was five, and growing up I didn't have any real desire to get married. I grew up around strong independent women and I was shaped by the 1990s era of girl power. Think Destiny's Child, TLC and the Spice Girls. Marriage wasn't completely foreign to me though. I was thirteen when my mum married my stepdad, the only wedding I could remember attending. For me, this only complicated matters though; it certainly didn't make marriage an aspiration.

When I became a Christian, I was surprised at all the talk of getting hitched and the sheer number of weddings that took place. In my new community, female independence wasn't championed in the way I'd become accustomed to. It was more manpower than girl power. It was also clear that some of the values I'd inherited didn't fit neatly in my new environment. Marriage was a coveted rite of passage that spoke of maturity – and singleness, it seemed, a sad and lonely existence for those in waiting. Across a number of faith communities, I observed a two-tier system that separated both camps giving preference to those who were wed and devaluing those who were running solo.

As I got older, I began to realise that wider society didn't actually differ much from these ideals either. They were certainly more pronounced in church circles, but people were still navigating the same issues of loneliness, a desire for companionship and starting a family. Love and romance were central and normative in my favourite sitcoms along with the 2.4 children to complete the picture. Beyoncé didn't need a man to pay her bills, but she still had Jay-Z.

As I write this chapter, twenty years later, I am now twelve years happily married with three beautiful children. To some, I have 'made it' and so my thoughts on singleness will be unwelcome and unrelatable. If you're single and reading this, I recognise that you've probably heard enough well-meaning married folk do a bad job of telling you how to live your life; that's not my goal here. Rather, I hope that, whether married or single, reading this chapter will help to remove some of the pressure that exists between us purely because of our relationship status.

The experiences of single people are not foregrounded in our communities, which often results in misunderstanding and invisibility. In her book, *Party of One*, Joy Beth Smith states that, 'Empathy, and sitting in the pain, naming it, is far more valuable than false comfort and clichéd advice.'[1] For our communities to truly be places where everyone feels like they belong, hearing the diverse stories among us is important. We don't take the pressure off by minimising our struggles, brushing them under the carpet and pretending things are ok. We take the pressure off by being honest, getting real and facing the facts. The pressure on singleness disempowers our communities in ways that impact us all – so where *does* it all come from? If you don't need a partner to be happy and fulfilled, why is there so much pressure to couple up?

The culture of coupledom

There's nothing wrong with desiring to be in a loving relationship – the Bible is clear that this is a good thing. However, many of us spend huge chunks of our lives as single people and struggle to be content. This is not necessarily because of our own internal lack of satisfaction though. It is often because of the feelings of shame and failure that we haven't lived up to the expectations of societal ideals or that we have even disappointed our family and peers. *The Single Friendly Church* survey reports that single people feel 'unwelcome, overlooked or misunderstood in family-focused churches'.[2] It's an uncomfortable reality, but marriage is idolised within our churches. Most celebrations revolve around family life – such as weddings and baby dedications – inadvertently excluding those who are single. Ministry leaders are usually couples, with the exception of the youth team, and platform speakers are rarely single. If they do buck the trend, they're most likely to be male. We don't often talk about our distrust of single people but a single youth pastor spoke to me about the reluctance she'd received from other youth pastors when trying to arrange meetings to collaborate and share best practice. She shared how on an occasion where her invitation was accepted, it turned out that the other pastor thought they were on a date!

The privileges of coupledom are not just experienced socially, but they permeate our laws, policies and come with an economic benefit too. In many cultures, marriage is a status symbol and singleness a handicap. This so often results in desperate attempts to mend a situation, which in reality may never have been broken in us. Maybe, the brokenness is out there.

Discussing the pressure she felt to get married and have children as she approached thirty, actress Emma Watson garnered attention by using the phrase 'self-partnered' to describe her happy and single status. Rather than succumbing to the pressure to find another partner, she chose to reframe singleness as a time for personal growth, which allowed her to focus on her relationship with herself. Similarly, influencers like Medina Grillo, author of *Home Sweet Rented Home*, are bucking the culture and using their platform to dispel the stigmas around renting, something that disproportionately affects single people because owning a house is often too big of a financial commitment for two, let alone one. More individuals are choosing to embrace the joys and autonomy of singleness through things like solo and group travel, but pressures surrounding a single status still persist.

Sexual dehumanisation

In society, being in a sexual relationship is believed to be fundamental to human existence. To be a virgin in adulthood is so radical that you're viewed as alien and immature, while being celibate is considered an impossible feat unless you're unwanted or in a state of recovery. Everyone, everywhere is talking about sex and how good it is, or at least how good it *should* be. From your favourite Netflix series, to the latest music release, it feels like everyone's *doing* it and you should be too. While typically the church teaches that sex outside of marriage is wrong, the culture teaches that it is necessary for wellbeing, inclusion and survival. It's no wonder then that we are conditioned to believe that our happiness is dependent on it.

Most of the polls report a growing trend in singleness, which reflects the reality that people are also marrying later or not at all. UK society is changing. Forty per cent of adults are single, half of whom are over the age of thirty-seven. According to the Office for National Statistics (ONS), the percentage of those in their forties who have never been married has doubled in the last twenty years. However, that statistic doesn't always correlate with sexual habits, so for the Christian single who wants to remain celibate until marriage, there is another degree of pressure. A friend in her thirties recently shared how difficult she finds the journey of celibacy. 'It is made more challenging because the culture and the church are sipping the same Kool-Aid. Both promote a narrative that to be truly human is to be in romantic relationships,' she said. In many senses, to be outside of a couple is to be on the margins. Counterculturally, actress and comedian Yvonne Orji has boldly shared about her commitment to celibacy as a woman in her thirties working in the entertainment industry. While the pressure of sex and marriage combined creates unhealthy standards that reinforce a sense of lack, Yvonne's openness and visible embrace of her womanhood is empowering for those choosing to abstain.

Whatever choices we make, it's important that they flow freely from our personal convictions and from grace, rather than external pressure to perform and to fulfil the expectations of others. It is not surprising that well-meaning people get wed prematurely or for the wrong reasons, only to end in the real brokenness of divorce a few years later. Holding ourselves to standards we don't believe in or feel unable to sustain can lead to resentment, hiding and harmful activity. For example, the harrowing revelation of sexual abuse by priests has often been linked to enforced celibacy. We have to be honest about where we're at and the uniqueness of our circumstances. Furthermore, while a loving marriage satisfies a healthy desire for sex, it does not remedy sexual immorality or struggles with our sexuality that can resurface after the 'I dos'.

In response to some of these pressures, more Christians are choosing to cohabit as a way to give themselves the chance to really get to know someone before tying the knot and to reduce financial burdens.

But what else might assist in our desire to choose grace? Is there any wisdom that can help us holistically as we seek to lighten the load? For Lauren Windle, author of *Notes on Love: Being Single and Dating in a Marriage Obsessed Church*, considering our relationship with Jesus is a helpful litmus test. 'It's fine to date, it's fine for it to be fun, it's fine for it to be painful at times, but it's not fine for it to pull you away from God,' she writes.[3] Centring our relationship with the Lord first helps us to live freely and make decisions that will serve us in the long term. Being aware of who is on the throne of our heart helps us to discern whether our pursuit of a potential new relationship is coming into conflict with our pursuit of the Lord. No two experiences of singleness are the same, so it's not helpful to compare ourselves with others. Furthermore, differences can also be seen starkly along the lines of gender.

Gender differences

While men are assigned the prefix of Mr, women traditionally have been given the choice of Miss or Mrs to denote their marital status, a signifier of adulthood. Historically they have been defined by their partners, relying on them for financial support and safety in the absence of opportunities for work and education. The stigmas associated with singleness have been hard to shake even in today's comparatively more feminist society, where beliefs about a woman's incompleteness outside of marriage still linger and are in fact reinforced. Furthermore, if marriage is the route to motherhood, then there's also the pressure of your biological clock. As a woman, society is systemised to make you feel like you're running out of time and, because there are fewer men than women in church, the numerical disadvantage for women associated with dating in the church adds further weight. According to my single female friends, dating in 2022, especially online, is a minefield. They've been love-bombed, felt the pressure to look on point at every turn, and have been left with the sense that the reality of who a guy turns out to be often falls short of the way they've represented themselves.[4] For the single woman who works and has perhaps bought a home of her own it is also all too easy for her to be seen as intimidating, too independent or not feminine enough. Friends have told me that they have been encouraged to 'dumb down' because guys might be intimidated by their success. Their accomplishments have thrust them into a space where not many single men live or are secure enough to embrace them.

There are far more women than men in the church, so I was surprised to hear from a male friend that he too felt it was hard to find a 'good woman'. He perceived a growing trend in females who say that they want a rich husband to take care of their needs so that they don't have to work. This expectation was described as both pressurising and unattractive. Furthermore, many men also feel the pressure of a hyper-masculine culture which can leave single Christian men feeling that they are less of a man if they're not getting in between the sheets. Another male friend described the pressure he feels to settle down because he wants his parents to see his kids before they get too old. He believes that deep down, most people want to start a love story and, in his opinion, it takes a special kind of person to want otherwise.

If a love story is the goal, then how do we take the pressure off while waiting for the story to begin? And if it's not, how can we ensure it doesn't erode our sense of worth?

Revaluing singleness

Ministries formed on the basis that singleness is a problem to be solved reinforce unhealthy narratives and can also add to feelings of discontentment and disunity. 'It is not good for the man to be alone' (Genesis 2:18) has unhelpfully been used to describe aloneness in the context of love relationships only and to increase the urgency of finding a partner. Single people are not impersonal monoliths – they have different circumstances and needs as widowed, divorced, separated, queer, single parents or young adults, for example. You can also be married, miserable and lonely so positioning marriage as a remedy to singleness is problematic on many levels.

An accurate reading of the Bible reveals that both marriage and singleness are gifts from God and neither is better than the other. The call to honour God with our bodies applies to both alike. Although marriage and procreation have been the norm since Genesis and children spoken of as a spiritual inheritance, the Apostle Paul wrote that because single people have more time to devote their lives to God, being unpartnered is actually prefer-able to marriage. I have often heard married people say that they struggle to be led by single people because they don't know what it's like to be married and have a nuclear family. While I under-stand this line of thinking and agree that life experiences differ and should be acknowledged, it was also Paul, a single guy, who wrote the majority of the New Testament, including the many teachings we have grown to appreciate on relationships. Jesus himself was fully human and unpartnered yet exemplified through the relation-ships with his closest friends and those whom he encountered what it means to love.

Wisdom and counsel that flows from the Spirit of God does not discriminate on the basis of our marital status. Our identity before God and our ability to hear his voice is the same. If there were any bias, it seems that the ability to be led by the Spirit is potentially greater for the single person because of the lack of distraction brought about from family life. 'An unmarried woman or virgin is concerned about the Lord's affairs; her aim is to be devoted to the Lord in both body and spirit' (1 Corinthians 7:34).

Many of Jesus' followers were single and the Bible even specifi-cally records the activity of single women. 'He had four unmarried daughters who prophesied' (Acts 21:9). How random that Luke would include this detail, how striking for a culture that viewed women as voiceless. It's a short sentence but Luke wanted us to know that Philip the evangelist had four single daughters who prophesied. It sounds just like the kingdom – revaluing those who have been cast aside. It is important for us to challenge the belief and, most significantly, the practice that infers single people have little to offer because it is most certainly rooted in culture, not the truth found in the canon of God's word or the life of Jesus. Challenging the assumption that married people are more impor-tant and making sure we open the door to friendships across our relationship status help to bridge the divide.

Key spiritual practice: Hospitality

My heart has been heavy at times listening to some of my single friends share their feelings of loneliness. Even if they are mostly content, many have shared the waves of sadness they feel – sometimes unexpectedly and, at other times, triggered by life events such as birthdays. Some have learnt that these intense feelings pass, and they try their best to lean into the love of family, friendships and God – but some have also shared their frustrations and the unhealthy ways they have sought to numb their desire for companionship in the short term. I have felt this heaviness most acutely talking to my queer friends and family who struggle to feel at home in the church. According to the British Red Cross, more than 9 million people in the UK say they often or always feel lonely at some point in their life.[5] Through work and study, many of us have moved away from our inter-generational support networks which provide the warmth of family and, according to the Office for National Statistics, we're less likely to have strong friendships or know our neighbours than residents anywhere else in the EU.[6]

Making room for the other and the unknown can be rare in our Western cultures, but the theme of hospitality runs throughout the whole Bible and serves as an example of inclusive practice in today's society. Although the Israelites were called to be exclusive in their worship of God and set apart from the way other nations lived, Yahweh wasn't exclusive in his love for them. The Lord commands the Israelites to look after the strangers and to treat them as natives because they themselves were once strangers in Egypt (Leviticus 19:34). His love and his plan for redemption extended beyond Israel and this was demonstrated in his instruction to ensure that outsiders felt welcome. In this sense, hospitality made them practise inclusivity and this idea of giving hospitality to strangers is continued into the New Testament.

We often have a view of hospitality that involves us rushing around and tidying frantically so we can welcome people into an immaculate home and sit them down to a perfect meal. It's easy to fuss over our guests without actually spending quality time with them. However, the story of Mary and Martha (Luke 10:38–42) teaches us that connection in the midst of chaos is better than no connection at all. Martha and Mary were two sisters who had the opportunity to host Jesus. While Martha busied herself in the kitchen to make sure that all the trimmings were taken care of, Mary chose to sit at his feet and be present. What is striking about this story is the way their special guest, Jesus, actually hosted Mary. In an environment where the culture told her she didn't belong, at the feet of the rabbi, he welcomed her. Martha was upset by Mary's failure to help, but Jesus said Mary had chosen the better way. Although Martha was acting in accordance with what was acceptable in her culture, Mary responded with the longing of her heart. She knew there was no need for respectability in the presence of Jesus and she chose connection over conforming to her cultural pressures. While Martha served the tradition, Mary gleaned wisdom from her Saviour.

When Aaron and I got married, we said that we wanted to have an open home. We wanted our house to be a place where people could come and feel like part of the family. You will often hear him say 'Mi casa su casa' to guests, especially if they're being overly polite. For the first few visits I don't mind getting you a drink, but I love it when someone feels comfortable enough to open the fridge and help themselves. Don't get me wrong I enjoy hosting friends and family well, beautifying the guest room if they're staying over and preparing a nice meal. But if every visit feels like a busy occasion needing lots of preparation, after which you collapse in an exhausted heap, it creates pressure and it's hard to settle into the ease, presence and authenticity of family.

Hospitality is not about convenience but delighting in welcoming others, embracing presence and sharing together. Our lives have often become so static that there is no room for others to move around them – and this can apply to us all. We lead busy lives but jam-packed schedules without any margin leave no room for this simple practice. I am an advocate for healthy boundaries, but if we create exclusive fortresses around our lives, we hinder the extent to which others can belong. Private hospitality was a high moral virtue in the first century, requiring the host to open their homes to travellers they didn't know. While it wouldn't necessarily be wise to let a random person stay at your home today, through our church communities we've had wonderful opportunities to experience this in a safe way. When we moved to Manchester, we were invited by a single mum at our church to stay in her two-bed apartment with her and her daughter. She gave up her room and slept on the couch so we could be comfortable. To this day, they are still like family to us. We attend our children's plays, babysit, have movie nights, celebrate promotions and eat together. The depth of our relationship today was initiated by her hospitality. On the flip side, we've also had the joy of hosting others for short and extended stays, usually single people who have become family friends.

I'll be honest and say that as a married person I have sometimes felt unwelcome in the lives of my single friends. Because of my distance from a single person's reality, I've been told that single women in particular will find it difficult to relate to me because we don't share the same struggles. This was uncomfortable but important for me to hear, to consider the ways in which I can be more responsive to the needs of my single friends. However, as I've shared, I have heard the exact same thing said in the reverse by married people. Does this mean then that married and single people are limited in the depths of relationships they can have together? When I read the Bible and I look at the changing nature of our communities, I am convinced that we need to move past these discomforts and divisions, to ask questions and have honest conversations that facilitate our unity. Questions like: Do I find ways to celebrate my single friends as well as my married ones? Do married and single people feel welcomed alike in my life? Who gets invited to parties and get-togethers? Do I think about the needs of my single friends? In what ways do I consider the needs of my married friends? Do I take the reduced availability of my married friends personally? In what ways am I making time to learn and receive from both married and single people? What assumptions and judgements do I make about people based on their relationship status?

I am incredibly grateful for my single friends who draw me into new spaces and often bring a sense of freedom and freshness to my life. Some are godparents to our children and have gracefully journeyed with me through the major transitions of marriage and motherhood. I know at times I have been so absorbed in my world that I have found it hard to even contemplate their reality. At other times, they have been unaware of the challenges of mine. However, hospitality helps us to bear with each other gracefully, it tends to our loneliness, and it invites new perspectives and a fuller experience of the body of Christ. Both single and married people serving, leading and teaching, can know that we are qualified by our willingness to sit at the Saviour's feet rather than our relationship status. Jesus constantly modelled inclusivity and his example reminds us that in rooms where the culture may say we don't belong or have nothing to contribute, we are always welcome because he has extended his invitation to us – and we're welcome to take the pressure off.

Let's take a pause and 'check in'. Look back at page 12 for some questions to help you reflect.

4

Pressure off purity

The only thing I remember my mom saying to me about sex was in passing one day while cooking dinner. My cousin was visiting, and she said to us both, 'All I'm saying, girls, is not before you're sixteen, not before you're sixteen, please.' We both laughed. I don't even know what prompted that remark, to be honest, but that was it. Friends have shared that their parents told them absolutely nothing about sex or the biology of reproduction. Some guys received no talks about wet dreams and some girls were not even spoken to about starting their menstrual cycle – a topic which continues to be taboo today even though all women go through it! I remember another conversation I had with my older sister in my late teens because I wanted to understand what sex felt like. What would happen during my first experience, and would it be painful? She happily talked me through what to expect.

However, my exposure to sex happened long before then. For example, in my primary years I remember being introduced to pornography at a family friend's house. Sex was all around, and beyond those two conversations there were few guidelines or stand-ards to inform how I engaged with it. From the music I listened to, the books I read and the sitcoms and films I watched, the world felt like a very sexual place, until I entered the church.

My experience at church was very different. No one talked about sex, unless to discourage you from having it before marriage. It was only spoken about in a negative sense and in terms of its danger, so in this environment, lots of people felt almost *asexual*. A friend shared with me that she doesn't remember ever being told she was beautiful or attractive in church. Psalm 139, which tells us 'you are fearfully and wonderfully made', was often quoted and spoke to her intrinsic value, but it wasn't the same. Pressure on purity meant there was no celebration of her femininity or her body, only a rejection of it and its desires.

In this new community, my own relationship with my body and how I chose to clothe it started to change: I traded the catsuits that my breasts tumbled out of as I moved vigorously on the dance floor for the decency of button-ups, knee-lengths and a song of praise. Looking back at twenty-year-old me, I was definitely a bit too old fashioned, but it fitted the bill. Furthermore, because of the over-exposure to sex I experienced growing up, I actually welcomed modesty and celibacy as an aspiration. In many ways it helped to dignify my body and develop a new narrative around my sexuality. It taught me that healthy sexual expression is not casual, nor is it cheap. It created space to explore what it meant to belong to Christ and honour him with my body. Especially as a woman, I felt it protected me from getting too involved emotionally with someone I didn't think was a keeper. It created an opportunity to build a relationship on the foundation of friendship and intimacy beyond sex. However, there was still a huge gap to bridge.

As touched on in the previous chapter, because sexual activity is often deemed central to human flourishing, many people believe that a lack of sex is an unhealthy denial of self. Even for many of us as Christians, abstinence is an outdated and unrealistic concept. Sex is increasingly casual, accessible and experimental, but we still struggle to have healthy dialogue about it, in and outside of the church. Conversations seem to fall into one of two camps – either salacious or super-sanctified. For the culture, anything goes as long as it's consensual. In the church, we don't want to talk about it at all. We are bombarded with sexual imagery even when we aren't looking for it, so pretending the elephant in the room isn't there only creates dissonance between our faith and our human reality.

But it turns out that a lack of boundaries and heavy censorship are just as harmful as each other. So what is the answer? Why is there so much pressure surrounding it and why does it affect us so much?

Purity culture

Part of the problem is that the idolatry of sex isn't just an issue for wider society, it exists in the church too. The negativity around sex and heavy emphasis on sexual purity have meant that some people start to believe that their failure to adhere to certain behavioural standards might affect their very salvation. It facilitates a culture of punishment rather than compassion and love; control rather than true discipleship.

Celibacy before marriage is an established teaching in the church. However, the modern-day purity culture began in the 1990s among evangelicals in the United States. It aimed to promote a biblical view of purity against the backdrop of rising rates of teen pregnancy and a rejection of traditional Christian values in society. Purity culture discouraged dating and premarital sex through tools such as purity balls, pledges and rings to encourage sexual purity. Women were taught to dress a certain way so as not to tempt men, and young people were discouraged from dating. This overemphasis on what young people were doing with their bodies had far-reaching effects and, although the movement has not been at the forefront of culture since the noughties, its impact can still be felt today.

Writing for The Conversation, Elle Thwaites, a PhD candidate in the UK, avers that:

The permeation of purity culture into church teachings and cultures can be seen in anxieties around male-female friend-ships, relationship expectations, the Christian idolisation of marriage, the equation of virginity with value, and inferences that women are responsible for gatekeeping men's sexual behaviour.[1]

The gender-based stereotypes within the movement were particularly harmful for women, whose bodies and sexual agency were oppressed, but they affected men too. A number of researchers have also found correlations between the themes intrinsic to purity culture and rape myth acceptance. While those who are deemed sexually pure are put on a pedestal of innocence, those who fall from these standards are shamed and more likely to be blamed if sexual assault takes place. Furthermore, in a culture that teaches women that their bodies exist for the pleasure of men, it fails to define consent, even within marriage.

At the height of the movement in 1997 came the popular book by Josh Harris called *I Kissed Dating Goodbye*, which has since received heavy criticism, including from the author himself who admits that:

In an effort to set a high standard, the book emphasized practices (not dating, not kissing before marriage) and concepts (giving your heart away) that are not in the Bible. In trying to warn people of the potential pitfalls of dating, it instilled fear for some – fear of making mistakes or having their heart broken. The book also gave some the impression that a certain methodology of relationships would deliver a happy-ever-after ending – a great marriage, a great sex life – even though this is not promised by Scripture.[2]

In 2017, Harris, who expressed that he no longer considers himself a Christian announced that he was separating from his wife Shannon and, just a week before he went public with the news, Shannon took to social media and posted,

My fundamentalist conservative Christianity experience taught me to ignore my inner voice. It's not possible to unpack this in one post, using one scripture or angle. But early on, I learned to distrust and override myself out of fear in an environment where those in authority held tremendous control over leaders and members.[3]

This erosion of the 'inner voice' meant that many individuals struggled to trust their own judgement and articulate their feelings, deepening the silent shame.

Similarly, in her book, *Red Lip Theology*, public theologian Candice Benbow shared the confusing teaching she received about 'soul ties' from the church.[4] Her acceptance of this idea ended after a service concluding 'Women's Month', where 'the co-pastor/first lady' invited the virgins to come and make a special offering to God 'with their pure bodies', making those who had a sexual past feel unworthy and ashamed.[5] In 2022, Beyoncé's single, 'Church Girl', gave voice to painful stories like these and empowered Black women especially to speak out, and to love and liberate their bodies. Reclaiming our voices and connecting with our bodies is important if the heavy shame attached to purity culture is to be shifted – and we need safe environments in which to do this.

A close Christian friend told me about her decision to have sex with a guy she was dating. It was a big decision for her to share this and I felt honoured that she was willing to reveal her vulnerability to me, but I was saddened to hear, months later, that she felt judged and condemned by me. Rather than being a non-judgemental place to explore her own values and decisions, our conversation had made her feel like she was doomed for hell. Through my questioning of her choices, my friend heard the voice of disappointment over and above the voice of love and acceptance. I took her words to heart. For someone who knows me so well, but also knows how much I treasure and respect them, this really hit home. Our interaction led her to feel more wary about sharing things that she thought I would disapprove of; she felt that it was no longer safe to do that. I apologised for the hurt that was caused, thanked her for sharing how she felt and let her know it wasn't my intention for her to feel that way. I have my own story and have so appreciated the voices of grace that have journeyed with me. I was sad that she hadn't felt that same grace in our conversation. It was a reminder that regardless of our stance on sexuality, it's important to approach these deeply personal issues with compassion and grace. The outcome of our chat was far from the reality of what I saw in the life of Jesus – people didn't leave him feeling condemned. The pressure my friend felt was probably bigger than our encounter – but it illustrates the vital truth that if someone is burdened with a lifetime of sexual shaming, it is essential that these conversations are handled with tremendous care.

Trauma responses

In her book *Pure*, author Linda Kay Klein says:

> You can't have internalised all of this deep sexual shame your entire life and then all of a sudden snap your fingers. You are taught to experience shame in association with your sexuality. Those neural circuits are fired together so often that eventually, just a thought about sex will automatically fire that shame neural circuit. Releasing all of that shame takes a tremendous amount of hard work. They need to deconstruct what they were taught, and rewire the brain to no longer see sexuality and spirituality as mutually exclusive.[6]

Our bodies often carry trauma in response to the stress that has been endured about our sexuality and this can continue into marriage too. Beyond the vows, many couples struggle with the transition from being bombarded with messages that sex is wrong to being told that it is now ok. Linda Klein grew up in the purity movement and spoke to *Elle* magazine about some of the problems it created.

> The purity culture not only teaches that you need to be utterly non-sexual before marriage, but that after marriage, you need to become extremely sexual. You need to be able to meet all of your husband's wants and needs. If you can't, that is seen as potentially dangerous – he could end up cheating, he could end up leaving. It's presented as an equation: If you're non-sexual before marriage, then you'll have a perfect sexual life after.[7]

This misogynistic attitude adds increased pressure for women as described by another friend of mine. After suffering from panic attacks whenever she tried to have penetrative sex in the first couple years of marriage, she shared that she struggled to separate sex from sin. Since overcoming these challenges, she decided to train as a sex therapist to help educate and support other Christians.[8] She explained how sex education in general has typically come from a male perspective and how this has influenced conversations about sex in society as a whole. For example, she shared how a recent survey highlighted that 40% of both men and women could not identify the clitoris, how we don't know our bodies and it is only in the last fifty years or so that we have begun to understand about female genitals, their size, etc. The truth is that we all have a sexual self and it is part of how God created us. She highlighted that we often support single men by assuming that it is normal for men to have sexual desire, whereas single women and widows can be excluded by the assumption that they are ok and, as a result, shame eats them up.

In her opinion, what is needed is better education about our bodies and our sexuality from a place of faith rather than fear. Fear avoids sex in the worry that if people find out it's pleasurable, they'll just do it casually. Faith recognises that God created sex and all the parts that make it amazing in a holistic way beyond the physical. Faith celebrates that God has created us for deep connection. Growing in our understanding of this helps to develop a healthy understanding of sex for us all. Even with the best intentions, concern born of fear can prevent us from preparing people for a safe and enjoyable sex life.

Into the grey

Against the backdrop of the harmful narratives that have emerged from our churches, the weight of the shame we feel in the area of our sexuality can become a barrier to our relationship with God and each other. When we are emotionally disconnected from people, it's easy to apply a blanket solution to a unique situation. However, when someone close to us is rejected by the status quo, we are moved to step into the grey and love in a very personal way. Conversations about consent and contraception should be normal in our communities. Emotional ties *are* deepened when we have sex, but it's important to avoid over-spiritualising and failing to take into account the complexities of someone's background in our conversations. This can be particularly harmful for those with a history of abuse. Erroneous teachings that disempower people and hold them in the past don't invite grace and need to be disrupted.

The sexual ethic that we need is not going to derive from the isolation of the pulpit or the academy, it will be hammered out in collaboration with the real lives of men and women in the pews. Men and women who deeply love God and desire to worship him in Spirit and truth. Our approach to discovering God's heart on a matter has to engage with our lived experience if it is to have meaning in our everyday lives. Isn't this what Jesus came to do? He put on flesh, he embodied our human reality so that he could identify with every struggle we would face. So that he could show us how to live, redeem our earthly bodies and point us to an eternal reality in him. So what else does the gospel say to us about purity?

Purity is often spoken about in terms of behaviour, what we can or cannot do. However, when we read Scripture in its entirety, we see that it is not centred on our sexual activity. We also see that we are purified as a result of receiving Christ (John 15:3). This is not credited to the quality of our life, it's about the quality of the blood of Jesus through whom we receive a new heart that produces in us godly desire and actions. The commitment to purity is for us all because our bodies belong to the Lord, and they are given with the primary purpose to worship him (1 Peter 2:9). Speaking in the Beatitudes, Jesus bypasses external behaviour to focus on the internal, inward part of our life and teaches, 'Blessed are the pure in heart, for they will see God' (Matthew 5:8). A pure heart is about undividedly loving the Lord above all else (James 4:4–8) and subsequently this posture results in our obedience. Living a life of purity, therefore, cannot be about trying to be good enough, lest we start performing all over again. When we shift the focus from our bodies and our doing to our being in God's presence and loving him wholeheartedly, that's when we find the grace to live holy lives.

Trying to unpick the complexities of how pressure on purity has uniquely distorted our reality is a painful task and not all of our communities are willing or equipped to engage in it. So where does that leave those of us who are hurting and searching for a new way? If it is God's will that we be sanctified and avoid sexual immorality (1 Thessalonians 4:3–4), what exactly does that mean for Christians today and what should it look like? What should we do when our emphasis on marriage as the remedy for sexual fulfilment and freedom has the potential to cause just as much harm in the church as the messages of sexual casualness in wider society? How do we remedy misogynistic teachings that have caused body shame and created fear around this beautiful God-given gift? How do we develop a sexual ethic that values the bodies and expression of both men and women? In light of our present struggles, how do we hold on to the truth that this life isn't all there is, that we are called to a life in the Spirit with an eternal hope? How do we respond if we identify as queer or same-sex attracted? And how do we treat our friends and family who do not align with our heteronormative expectations? It is clear that both the church and society at their extremes have given us a broken sexual ethic. Neither allows us to live into our identity in Christ or as his beloved community and we're still searching for the answers.

Key spiritual practice: Compassion

Taking the pressure off purity requires us all to take a look in the mirror and consider the ways that we may be perpetuating or contributing to harmful narratives that hinder the reception of grace.

It took a while to settle on a spiritual practice for this chapter, in part because I don't want to offer cheap encouragement for an area that is filled with pain, and also because I recognise that there are times when I have got my response to this conversation badly wrong. I feel there is still so much room for learning and growth in this area for me personally and I know many of you will feel the same. What I believe we really need at this time in the conversation on purity, however, is to be heard without judgement. For this reason, I have chosen to encourage us towards the spiritual practice of compassion, which literally means 'to suffer together'. While empathy refers to our ability to take on the perspective and feel the emotions of another, compassion is when those thoughts and feelings are met with a desire to help. In other words, after listening we are moved into action.

Practising compassion leads us to listen and understand how, often unintentionally, our church communities have been harmful places for those who genuinely seek to honour Christ with their bodies. We listen to hear the stories of rejection from those who were abused, back-benched and shunned. To hear the struggles of those who have felt disempowered by the double emphasis of both marriage and sex. To hear the pain of those whose reality has been so changed by their negative experience in the church, that to show up in a faith community context is now far too triggering and traumatic. When we practise compassion, we sit in uncomfortable spaces and bear witness to the heartfelt experiences of others before offering our thoughts, advice or solutions. We consult with those who have suffered and together ask God to help us move forward more lovingly.

Passing in front of Moses, the first word the Lord uses to describe himself is *compassionate*. 'The LORD, the LORD, the compassionate and gracious God, slow to anger, abounding in love and faithfulness' (Exodus 34:6). The Hebrew word for it is *rahum* and it paints a picture of a mother's tenderness towards her baby. It's patient, nurturing, selfless and attentive. It is this tenderness that results in Jesus' entry into the world and throughout his life he consistently demonstrates compassion for the vulnerable and the sick. He is deeply moved – and he encourages us towards the same.

> You must be compassionate, just as your Father is compassionate. Do not judge others, and you will not be judged. Do not condemn others, or it will all come back against you. Forgive others, and you will be forgiven.
> (Luke 6:36–38, New Living Translation)

Our ability to extend compassion and empathy into the lives of others is closely linked to our ability for self-compassion. When the religious leaders brought a woman caught in the act of adultery to Jesus, they argued that she should be stoned as according to the law but they wanted to know what he would do in this instance. Jesus responded, 'Let any one of you who is without sin be the

65

first to throw a stone at her' (John 8:7). One by one the stones fell to the ground as the leaders walked away. Jesus didn't condemn this woman to death and from his questioning, it is clear that, in the eyes of God, her sin was no different to the sin of the religious leaders who praised themselves for their piety. Turning to her on the ground where she lay, probably terrified and in great distress, Jesus asked her; 'Woman, where are they? Has no one condemned you? "No one, Lord," she answered. "Then neither do I condemn you," Jesus declared. "Now go and sin no more"' (John 8:10–11).

Only God can righteously judge, and one day he will, but again and again he chooses to show us his compassion. When we follow Jesus, he leads us to extend this compassion to each other. Purity culture has a tone of superiority, but compassion kneels down in humility. Purity culture points the finger, but compassion acknowledges that we are all sinners in need of a saviour. Purity culture condemns, but compassion flows from grace with the selfless desire to heal and restore. Pressure off!

Let's take a pause and 'check in'. Look back at page 12 for some questions to help you reflect.

5

Pressure off marriage

I'd like to say that we had it all down pat when we got married but in honesty, my husband and I refer to the first couple of years of marital 'bliss' together as World War III. Sure, we had great times during that period but behind the scenes it was *full* of pressure.

As soon as we'd crossed the threshold into marriage, I felt out of control. We moved into a small two-bedroom flat which provided no escape in times of disagreement and a cycle of frustration and negative exchanges began. If something didn't go the way I thought it should, I refused to let up. I couldn't allow Aaron to think I was a fool or some kind of doormat. I needed to put my foot down in case this created problems in the future. I didn't choose my battles; I fought *every* battle. I wanted to remain in control because I didn't want to get hurt. What I didn't realise is that while I was busy self-preserving, I was unable to open myself up to the love we both wanted to experience. We were both stubborn and it didn't work, it didn't make us happy.

There were times during an argument when I would look at Aaron and be thinking: *I know you love me and I love you, but in this moment, we just can't get it together!* Two worlds had collided, and we didn't have the tools to navigate our new normal. I stopped swearing when I became a Christian and I started again in marriage! We were tossing coins for the washing up and arguing over stuff we'd forget even happened three days later. The morning after a big argument (which involved me throwing shoes across the bedroom), I broke down crying; I didn't recognise myself. Aaron went to the cricket. Later, we arranged to meet up with a couple whom we respected. We told them what had happened and, even recalling the event, I still couldn't find an alternative in my mind other than to go flip mode! I was scared. Because marriage is put on a pedestal in the church, it can surprise people who are single, dating, engaged or indeed married to know that it's actually really hard at times. Unknowingly, choosing to love the one I loved, day in, day out, would not be as easy as I thought. So, chaos aside, how *do we* develop healthy expectations about marriage?

Till death do us part

It's been described by some as a fairy-tale (think Disney circa 1990s) and by others as a prison sentence, but let's face it, neither of these analogies are helpful preparation for a lifelong commitment. If we romanticise marriage, we will feel like we've failed and that something is wrong when the reality of our vows sets in. Normal bumps in the road can feel like huge mountains that make us want to give up. It may also reduce our willingness to seek help if it's needed, because we feel shame. A healthy marriage is not always about having fun with your best mate, sometimes it's about enduring the mundane with someone you're struggling to see eye to eye with. On the other hand, when we give our marriages a death sentence, we can become passive and apathetic. We can feel hopeless and fatalistic when pressures hit and accept less than what we are both desiring. In worst-case scenarios, we may tolerate abusive situations. The sense of hopelessness may lead us to avoid seeking help when we need it. The pressure is still on.

While the definition of marriage itself is under debate, it has been said that millennials are changing their approach to marriage, in part because of their own childhood experiences. This is resulting in less traditional routes to 'Mr and Mrs' if they choose to wed at all. As I've shared, marriage was not something I aspired to growing up but rather a desire that grew slowly after salvation so I can definitely relate to the current trends as highlighted by an Insider article:

> Often the children of divorce themselves, millennials tend to fear going through one. So, they're being strategic when it comes to love. They're taking more time to find the right partner, cohabiting before legally committing, and signing prenups to protect their assets. As a result, they're bringing the divorce rate down.[1]

Whether your vision of marriage is Jasmine and Aladdin or HMP, you're going to experience pressure. Two imperfect people rubbing shoulders every night are bound to experience tension, that's normal. But those tension points will be different for everyone because every relationship is different. There's no 'one size fits all' – in fact, one of the greatest sources of pressure is the many misconceptions about what our marriages 'should' be like. With the help of an Instagram poll, I thought it was worth calling some of them out from the start.

'Disney' expectations
- Having children improves your marriage
- You can change your spouse
- Marriage should be easy, and you shouldn't argue
- You are both responsible for each other's happiness
- Your spouse should be your best friend
- Getting married will solve problems of trust and insecurity
- Marriage will complete you
- Your social life can remain unchanged
- Happy couples do everything together
- The man should be the main breadwinner and the woman the domestic goddess

'HMP' expectations

- Marriage counselling is a sign of failure
- Monogamy and marriage = boring sex
- Two Have Become One, so you're no longer individuals
- People don't change – a leopard never changes its spots
- We can't go out or on holiday individually or with our friends
- Women don't enjoy sex as much as men
- Even if my marriage is abusive, I should stick it out
- Keep a secret stash of cash just in case
- It's the woman's job to tend to her husband's sexual needs so he doesn't stray
- In-law relationships are burdensome

None of these myths about marriage have a sound biblical foundation. Most of them are cultural or based on different people's opinion and individual experiences. Cultural preference and opinions, even when shared with our spouse, do not have within them the ability to produce the kind of marriage that God desires for us. They may help to inform our decisions but, when we build on them, we construct in our own strength. We lean on our own understanding and bypass grace. Jesus' first miracle took place at a wedding ceremony. He honoured the institution of marriage with his presence. He turned water to the finest wine, bringing jubilation to the wedding guests – but today there seems to be so much pressure on this God-blessed institution.

Breaking the bank

According to the wedding website, Hitched, the average wedding cost in the UK in 2021 was £17,300.[2] If you think that's a lot, pre-pandemic their annual survey revealed that in 2019, the figure was £31,974! For those of us with cultural traditions that may require us to celebrate across a few days and invite a host of unknown extended family and friends (by referral of your parents), we may consider these figures the starting line.

It's probably no surprise that one of the areas of recent increase in the budget is photography. A recent National Wedding Survey[3] found that almost 50% will go over their budget, and many have shared the pressure they feel to ensure that their pics are 'Instaworthy'. It doesn't just start on our wedding day though. The bended knee moment of our marriage proposals are now movingly captured in HD followed by engagement shoots and expensive hen and stag dos. Before you've even walked down the aisle to get wed, the pressure is on. I love romance and wedding celebrations though and, in many ways, the communal nature of large gatherings helps to bring honour and point to the common good of marriage beyond the couple themselves. Healthy marriages are good for society, but if we're in debt before we've walked down the aisle and we have no house in which to live, what good is that, especially when money problems are cited as one of the major causes of divorce? According to multiple sources, this expected financial burden is putting people off getting married altogether, but maybe the pressure surrounding the big day is more about our idolisation of the 'mystical union' into which we are entering. Marriage takes work – consistent and intentional work.

Learning a new way

Aaron and I both had to learn to grow in vulnerability in order to love and receive love – even when it hurts. Through a combination of talking, reading and praying, I began to talk to the Lord (rather than complain to Aaron) about things I was unhappy about and find grace to demonstrate my love in ways I knew he would appreciate. On one occasion I followed the challenges in a book called, *The Love Dare*, at times with great difficulty![4] After just a few days he noticed something was different about me. I chose to keep loving even when he was being negative, and the result was astounding. As I focused on improving my own actions rather than focusing on Aaron's mistakes, the very things that I had been fighting for – for months – would happen without me asking. The level of joy and laughter in our home increased and so did our expression of love to each other.

Twelve years later, I can tell you that we aren't perfect and still have so much to learn. We are still being formed and, as far as lifelong marriages go, in many ways we're babies. As our faith has matured, however, so has our understanding of each other. We've used tools like personality tests to better appreciate who we are, our strengths and weaknesses. Remembering that both of us are created in the image of God and that we belong to him affirms our value. We are precious and although we may not meet it all the time, it helps to uphold a standard in our treatment of each other. When we got married, one of our mentors encouraged us that our job was to help bring out all that God had put in each other. Understanding that God has purpose in each one of us helps us to see our marriage as a nurturing environment to live out from, not just in. If it is not producing freedom and flourishing for all then we must question if we are building our bonds on Christ.

Creating new boundaries

Another major pressure comes from the fact that a new marriage requires a shift in the boundaries of other significant relationships. The marriage unit is now superior to parental relationships (Genesis 2:24) and relationships with children who will one day grow up and leave for adult life. It is so easy to get lost in parental duties, especially when our children are young. However, if relationships with children take priority over the union that brought them into existence, it can put a strain on intimacy and friendship. Furthermore, when couples allow family members to involve themselves in their affairs, it can open the door to a whole host of problems that can damage their union.

Contract vs covenant

In line with the growth in prenuptial agreements, reality TV and the ease of divorce, marriage today is increasingly viewed as a contract rather than a covenant. Although these two words are used interchangeably at times, they are significantly different. Whereas a contract is a temporary agreement founded on mistrust, conditions and compromise, a covenant is intended to be permanent, for better or worse, unconditional and sacrificial. A contract is made between two people and the terms laid out so that each individual can seek their own best interests in an attempt to self-preserve. Failure to meet these terms results in the contract ending. However, a covenant is made between a couple and God, publicly, and it is marked by the giving of oneself in service. Failure to meet the terms is forgiven and parties keep no record of wrongs. It seeks the best interests of the collective rather than the individual.

When the Pharisees asked Jesus if it was lawful for a man to divorce his wife, Jesus referred to the Genesis account of creation (2:21–24) by saying, 'At the beginning the Creator made them male and female', adding, 'So they are no longer two, but one flesh' (Matthew 19:4, 6). Jesus was asserting that just as the body is one piece and cannot be whole if torn apart, so it is with marriage. The couple have entered a covenant, a sacred moral agreement where the terms are set by God. Jesus goes on to add those famous words, 'What God has joined together let no one separate.' A correct understanding of the purpose of marriage and what we are engaging in from the outset helps to safely shape our expectations around the stability of godly values.

In the new covenant (in the New Testament), marriage is a redemptive picture of the mystery of the Lord's relationship with the church. It is the earthly image of Christ's permanent oneness with us. We – the church – are called the bride and body of Christ. We are the beloved, the ones he chose to lay down his life for with no guarantee that we would return his affection. He has pursued us from the beginning of time and although he has been broken-hearted by our rejection time and time again, he refuses to give up on us. There is no greater love than this, it conquers our fears and creates space for connection and acceptance. For freedom and flourishing. It is with this picture of radical love that we frame our expectations of marriage and understand its purpose. Through our vows we enter a 'holy matrimony' and declare our exclusivity to our partners, as we have declared our devotion to the Lord.

In a wedding sermon written from his prison cell for his niece, theologian Dietrich Bonhoeffer wrote, 'It is not your love that sustains the marriage, but from now on, the marriage that sustains your love.'[5] At times, our commitment to our vows has held Aaron and me together when the belief in our ability to love one another was absent. We try our best to communicate with honesty, work through our stuff and we decided long ago that we would not throw around threats of divorce. We could choose to either stay together and be miserable, or stay together in love. We always choose the latter, if not straight away, eventually! Sometimes new challenges emerge but each year, as we choose to bask in the highs and work through the lows, we deepen our commitment. If it was only a contract, we could have both checked out years ago. However, knowing that we are submitted to each other and the covenant we made before God creates security.

Mutual submission

Getting my head around submission has taken some time, not just because of my understanding of the Bible's position on marriage but because of the way men and women are often pitted against

74

each other in society and the church. Many married and single women are still treated like second-class citizens because of cultural norms and misunderstandings of various teachings about female submission that are used to silence and affirm a husband's control over a wife. While the image of marriage was broken in Eden, in Christ, it is redeemed and restored by grace. Jesus pointed to the first marriage between Adam and Eve, which was one of partnership between diverse equals, not hierarchy, while Paul's teaching in Ephesians 5:21–33 is a picture of loving headship not dominance. It is a call to redeem godly leadership in the home because, as Nancy Pearcey comments:

> In ancient culture, many marriages were not love based. Spouses were selected with an eye to things like social status, property rights, and legal heirs. In sharp contrast, the New Testament taught men to 'love their wives as their own bodies.' The husband's 'headship' was redefined as self-sacrifice, modeled on Christ's sacrificial love.[6]

Biblical headship is about living a crucified life, it's not about control. It is about a husband loving sacrificially in order to live into this redemptive picture. While the couple's unity and oneness does not equal sameness, like the body made up of many parts, each brings something different to the unit in partnership, working together for a common goal. The message is clear, submission on either side should not lead to abuse (Colossians 3:19).

In true Aaron style, when I asked for a few thoughts on marriage, he summarised them very concisely by saying: *It's got to be intentional and it's a give and take.* Honest conversations are essential and so are support networks for times when things get challenging. The biggest pressure for him has been understanding himself and his own weaknesses, having to deal with his own past and the lack of modelling of what a good husband looks like. The biggest revelation, he said, is that you can sometimes be right but wrong. In other words, you can say the right thing the wrong way. He said it's got to be win–win in communication so resentment doesn't build. One of the places resentment does commonly build in marriages however, is in the bedroom, – often because someone feels unfulfilled or uncomfortable in their sex life. So what do you do if sex is underwhelming, infrequent or non-existent? How do you know that you're sexually compatible if you've chosen to wait?

When we got engaged we agreed to remain celibate until we got married as part of our desire to honour God in our relationship. Aaron hadn't grown up in church either and neither of us were virgins, but after reading the Bible and hearing the many teachings about sexual immorality, we believed this was God's best for our lives. Sexual intimacy was a gift to each other and reserving it for our wedding night felt like a way of expressing its value. It was tough because we dated for three years before the big day, but we did it and both agree that it was the right decision for us.

After we were wed, I was warned by a church leader never to discuss my sex life with anyone because it's such a private and intimate part of my relationship with my husband. While I understand and appreciate the importance of not casually inviting people into our bedrooms, where do we go when we need to explore our questions or speak to someone about our sexual challenges? It's hard to find the healthy in-between. There is a lot of pressure on newlyweds to have an incredible sex life from the get-go and some people argue that because sex is such an important part of our relationships we need to 'try before we buy', to ensure compatibility and avoid disappointment. The Bible teaches however, that 'The marriage bed must be a place of mutuality – the husband seeking to satisfy his wife, the wife seeking to satisfy her husband' (1 Corinthians 7:3, *The Message*). This call to mutual submission and love, leads us to yield our bodies with our focus on the pleasure of our partner.

As discussed, this was massively countercultural because in the Greco–Roman world a man's sexual freedom was normalised, but in Christ they were called to exclusivity as much as women. When we follow Christ, we see that in marriage, the language of care is no longer 'my' but 'our', and this posture massively helps us to reorient our focus and grow in our sex lives too. We have found that as we've learned more about each other, it is this mutual desire to serve and satisfy each other above all else that enables our sex life to thrive. We have gone through peaks and troughs especially as we've journeyed through pregnancy, breast-feeding and health issues but we love sex and it's an important part of our marriage. It's fun and explorative. Beyond the physical pleasure, it is a place of deep emotional and spiritual connection that embodies our union. It's healing and restoring and, in line with the growth of our relationship, like learning a language, it gets better and better. So, whether your first night is overwhelmingly orgasmic or a complete car crash, be encouraged because you have a lifetime to nurture your sex life together! If sex is not as frequent or as enjoyable as you would like, or it's ground to a halt, there is grace and help to redefine what you both want this wonderful gift to look like. Whatever the area of focus, sometimes inviting the new in marriage requires us to wipe the slate clean and start over.

Key spiritual practice: Forgiveness

No one knows me better than Aaron. He has the privilege of seeing the good, the bad and the downright ugly. He sees me at my most vulnerable which means he also knows my weaknesses and how to push my buttons. While this may not be intentional, when we are hurt by our spouse, the wounds go deep. In the Greek, the word forgiveness literally means 'to let go', to not take payment for a debt. It is God's love that sent Jesus to the cross for our debts and it is his forgiveness that allows the bride of Christ to enjoy a special relationship with the Lord. Through Christ's example as the bridegroom, we see that marriage is about sacrificial love, trust and a commitment to forgiveness is core to the success of our relationship with God and each other.

For believers, forgiving others is a command that is tied to our own forgiveness. 'For if you forgive other people when they sin against you, your heavenly Father will also forgive you. But if you do not forgive others their sins, your Father will not forgive your sins' (Matthew 6:14–15). When we allow offence to grow in our hearts, the fruit is ugly. It can result in revenge-seeking behaviour, ill health and have a negative impact on our marriage. We continue to give more power to the negative events and allow them to affect our future. It makes us bitter and causes us to hold grudges, which block the path of happiness and joy in our lives. Yet the Bible encourages us to, 'Get rid of all bitterness, rage and anger, brawling and slander, along with every form of malice. Be kind and compassionate to one another, forgiving each other, just as in Christ God forgave you' (Ephesians 4:31–32).

Marriage milestones aren't just about celebrating years of happy memories but also years of relearning, unlearning and difficult conversations. Sometimes we have to forgive *ourselves* so that our yesterday, which is long gone and unchangeable, is no longer free to dictate our lives today. When Peter asked Jesus how many times he should forgive his brother, thinking that seven times was in excess of the three times that was taught by the Rabbis in accordance with Amos 1:3–13, Jesus responds 'seven times seventy' times. In other words, because of the grace working through us by the empowerment of the Holy Spirit, there is no number to put on how many times we ought to forgive. Choosing to forgive does not minimise or justify the wrong. It didn't for Jesus, who still had to endure the cross. However, it opens the door to repentance and reconciliation.

I used to believe that I didn't need to forgive until the person who wronged me apologised. However, in Christ I see a higher way in his forgiveness of us while we were yet sinners. Nevertheless, we can sometimes get into the habit of saying sorry without changing our actions. This creates pressure in our marriages because it erodes confidence and trust. Repentance includes a sincere acknowledgement of the pain we have caused followed by turning away from negative behaviour. If we are desiring to live together in unity, it is something that we ought to take very seriously.

Jesus gives very few grounds for divorce, but he promises an abundance of grace for when we need it most. The wedding he attended had run out of wine and it would have been a big embarrassment to the family if this was not remedied. Thousands of years later and we are still scrambling to deliver our lavish celebrations! Jesus doesn't condemn the family or tell them they should have invited fewer people, but instead delivers the finest wine of the night. The wedding guests are blown away, the family are praised for saving the best till last and Jesus gets the glory. Like this wedding, sometimes our marriages feel like they are running out of wine, like they are lacking joy and love. The quality wine that we started with has run out and we don't even have any of the average stuff left. Like the process of fermentation, it takes years to build a marriage. While we endeavour to keep the wine in steady supply, inevitably there are times when we struggle. What we do have in plenty is the living water of the Holy Spirit. We may start with our best efforts, but each day, and especially when the wine is running low, we can ask him to help us forgive and love again.

Marriage provides companionship and it is a source of joy. When it functions as God intended, it sanctifies us and makes us holy. This is not something we can attain in our own might, but when we come to Jesus, he enables it to fulfil its ultimate purpose of glorifying God. Supernaturally, he makes our marriages richer than we ever could do in our own strength and he takes the pressure off.

Let's take a pause and 'check in'. Look back at page 12 for some questions to help you reflect.

6

Pressure off parenting

We were thrilled when we found out I was pregnant. We stopped fighting over the dish duties and, after almost five years of being married, we felt ready to introduce a child into the mix. A couple of weeks later the smiles faded as I came to blows with the first trimester. It was a shock to the system, but maybe that was God's way of preparing us for the adventure that is parenting – because, philosophically, very little has changed from those first twelve weeks. It's exciting, we continue to push through the sea of advice to find our own style, to feel out of our depth, to be thrown into unexpected twists and turns, to apologise to one another as it seemingly brings out the worst in us and rejoice in the beautiful moments that take our breath away.

It's important to acknowledge that not everyone is able or desiring to be a parent, which can be a source of great pressure for a variety of reasons. Furthermore, a romanticised view of parenting can be a weight for us all, including wider family members, carers and those involved in nurturing children. I know that as parents of three energetic young boys, one thing my husband and I didn't anticipate was just how intense and exhausting it can be. Nor did we know that we were going to be caught up in such an extraordinary wave of societal expectations about how we should fulfil our roles.

Regardless of where you find yourself on your journey with parenthood – in, out, or somewhere in between – I hope this chapter will help you to identify and acknowledge some of the key pressures you or those you love may encounter, and to relieve some of the excess pressure that we're collectively feeling.

Intensive parenting

Over the past fifty years there has been a shift in attitudes towards parenting which can be traced back to how the word 'parent' is used. From the 1970s, the word started to gain widespread use as a verb – to parent. In other words, it went from being something you *are* to something you *do*. Ring any productivity bells?! Author Jennifer Senior humorously describes the vast amount of parenting books on offer today as 'overwhelming – it's a giant, candy-colored monument to our collective panic'.[1] It's true. Choosing to raise a whole other human being is one of the biggest responsibilities we can ever have and can also be one of the most anxiety-inducing ones too. The 1980s saw what was called 'helicopter parenting', or overprotective parenting, come to the fore but the most dominant model today in the UK, US and Australia is described as 'intensive parenting'. A *New York Times* article entitled 'The Relentlessness of Modern Parenting' explains how it arose in the 1990s and 2000s following, 'A major shift in how people saw children. They began to be considered vulnerable and mouldable – shaped by their early childhood experiences – an idea bolstered by advances in child development research.'[2] In the same article, author Dr Hays is quoted as saying that this resulted in a parenting style that was 'child-centered, expert-guided, emotionally absorbing, labour intensive and financially expensive'. Jennifer Senior remarks that this has thrust parents into unchartered territory vacant of any 'rules, scripts or norms'.[3] There are so many decisions, so many unknowns – and no manuals. The article states that 'the relentlessness of modern-day parenting has a powerful motivation: economic anxiety'. Parents want to ensure their children have social mobility and that's reflected in our spending and over-scheduling as we try to get them 'ahead'. The amount of money we spend used to peak when they were in high school but is now highest when they are under six and over eighteen, leading people to reduce the number of children they have. Considered a norm for the white, upper-middle-class families, research shows that, 'People across class divides now consider [intensive parenting] the best way to raise children, even if they don't have the resources to enact it.'[4] Whether you're able to afford the costs associated with intensive parenting or not, the pressure is on.

Intensive parenting leads to high levels of stress for children too. Educator Julie Lythcott-Haims aptly called it a 'check-listed childhood' in her brilliant TED Talk.[5] The *New York Times* article also notes that, 'Research has shown that children with hyper-involved parents have more anxiety and less satisfaction with life, and that when children play unsupervised, they build social skills, emotional maturity and executive function.'[6] With each child you tend to relax a bit more, which probably contributes to why the last child is often more free-spirited (wild!) than the first. Furthermore, while our parenting has grown more intense, our communities have grown more divided. Increased mobility from study and work means that the inter-generational support traditionally available from family members is less accessible for many people today. Not only are we doing more – but we're doing more on our own. Aaron and I have both moved away from our home towns so we relate to this dynamic. It can be hard to catch your breath, especially when you're holding down a career.

Working parenthood

Alongside these cultural shifts, we've also seen an increase in the number of women returning to work after having children – sometimes for financial reasons and sometimes for the sanity of adult interaction. While some of us love getting down on the floor to do crafts every day, attending baby groups and going for cake with fellow parents, others of us are itching to get back to the working world because we thrive on the stimulation and rhythm of our working life. We enjoy contributing to wider society but that doesn't mean we want to burn out because of it. While legislation differs across the globe, in the UK and the US it's at its worst. Fathers often get minimal time off following the birth of a new-born. The cost of childcare, along with the pressure to work as though you have no children as well as looking after them as though work doesn't exist, is exasperating. Working parents can expect to pay almost two-thirds of their salary on childcare for their under two-year-old in the UK.[7] In the US, they can expect no paid leave or childcare support at all. According to recent research, biomarkers for chronic stress are 18% higher in working mums, rising to 40% when they have two children. And contrary to the belief that this is remedied by flexible working conditions, the study found that the real solution was to work less.[8] Unfortunately, working less is not a privilege afforded to all. But what is it exactly that constitutes *work*?

Many parents would argue that it is mentally and physically more challenging to be at home full time than to re-enter the working world, a feeling that was reinforced to great effect when we all turned into home schoolers during the global pandemic! UK Charity Pregnant Then Screwed is seeking to rectify what they call the 'motherhood penalty'. They argue that:

Mothers are forced out of the labour market by an economy that does not recognise the value of the unpaid care they provide. There are specific mechanisms that underpin our economy – childcare, parental leave policies and working patterns – that reinforce gendered stereotypes about who performs care and lead to a gender pay gap and low participation by mothers in the labour market.[9]

The contribution made by stay-at-home parents is not recognised, although, according to 2019 data from Salary.com, it equates to a median annual salary of $178,201 (around £140,000).[10] Being a stay-at-home parent can also be one of the loneliest jobs in the world and, contrary to the stigma of it being a luxury, many of these parents navigate a loss of identity and a decline in their mental health in the process.

Unfortunately, gendered parenting stereotypes are often compounded in our churches, where women do most of the volunteering alongside their work and family commitments. In exchange for a spiritual blessing, they are worn down and still have to pick up the slack when they go home. In paid ministry, wives often come as a 2-for-1 package alongside their salaried husbands. A decision from a man and/or a woman to reduce their involvement in their church community can often be seen negatively and as an unwillingness to prioritise ministry. On top of the pressures they may be facing, they can be made to feel that they are failing to prioritise God – rather than it being seen as a positive decision to prioritise family and avoid burnout. What if we were more honest about the fact that the utopia of merging family with church ministry has actually resulted in more marriage breakdowns and disenfranchised children than we'd like to admit? While we enjoy serving together and teaching our children the value of Christian community, when our service at church comes at the cost of the peace in our homes it's probably time to make some revisions. When we compartmentalise our public ministry and prioritise it over the health of our private family life, we create pressure. I believe we *can* occupy all of these spaces well when we do it in order: God, family, work. This helps us grow in integrity as Jesus taught and it helps us to move in grace. It's important to recognise that our various family circumstances often have different needs and time commitments. This will also vary through the different seasons of life. So how do we practically change our rhythm when we're so tired and short on time?

It takes a village

After we had our third child, I asked a friend how she navigated life with three children and she responded, 'Get help!' She was right. In spite of distance, we work hard at maintaining connection with grandparents, cousins, aunts, uncles and godparents and have been so thankful for the support of our church community and the friends who have become family over the years. They have cooked for us after the birth of our children, we've swapped date nights with other couples, and our parents have had the boys for extended stays so that Aaron and I can go away. We've also looked after our friends' children for their breaks and have enjoyed travelling with other families too. Parenting is not something we do alone, it really does take a village and community is part of God's design for our lives.

While it often feels like the demands and decisions are endless, throughout generations the Lord's expectations of us as parents haven't changed, nor has the promise of his grace. I believe our core responsibilities as parents can be found in the Bible: to love, to lead and to let go.

A biblical perspective

To love (Psalms 127:3)

Whether biological or not, God has given children to us as a gift and, as with any gift giving, there is an expectation that the receiver will cherish and look after it. Looking at the Lord as our example, we are called to listen to our children, protect them, pray for them, champion them and celebrate them – the way he does us. Our love affirms their value and significance in the world and helps to bridge a loving relationship for them with their heavenly Father too.

To lead (Proverbs 22:6)

As parents it's our job to train, discipline and nurture children so they can grow to become mature adults. They are watching and learning from us all the time and through our actions we model how to relate to ourselves and others. It is our responsibility to teach them about Jesus, first and foremost by example, teaching them about God's word so they can grow in grace for themselves. We can help to create an atmosphere of faith in the home, but it is the Lord who does the saving.

To let go (Mark 10:13–16)

People brought their children to Jesus to bless them, and we continue this tradition today through baby dedications and Christenings. We pray and ask the Lord to help us love and lead but also to let go of our children, recognising that one day they will need to fly the nest and fulfil their own purpose. Therefore, we *dedicate* them back to him. This is not a one-time event followed by a party and some cake, but a lifelong commitment that releases them to God, reminds us of our dependence on him and helps us to parent from grace rather than in our own strength. Sometimes letting go is tough but it requires us to trust that what we've put in them is enough, that their heavenly Father watches over them wherever they go, and they are safe in his care. It helps them to grow in confidence and independence too.

Having explored the origins of some of the societal pressures we face, we can understand why parenting with these virtues in our western reality is much easier said than done, even in the church. Granted I've only been in the game for eight years, but throughout it's been evident that, for most of us, our desire to do our best as parents sits against the backdrop of a steady stream of messages telling the story that we are not enough, we are not doing enough, and we don't have enough. In response, we try to be perfect, do and buy more unnecessary stuff, inadvertently inviting our children into the grand narrative.

Children see and children do. In turn they also struggle with the unworthiness born of perfectionism, with a lack of confidence because they've been wrapped in cotton wool, and with the insatiability of consumerism because they've been given so much. Then we criticise our mini-mes for lacking resilience, lacking initiative and being entitled. Sound familiar? As millennials and Gen Z, we've also been called spoiled, entitled, lazy, and failures at what's come to be known as 'adulting'. Rather than trying to perfect and improve our way through like everything else, maybe it's time that we commit to ruthlessly transforming the way we do parenthood?

Don't ask Google

While many of the insights from child-development research have been for the better, what we also need is a return to trusting our bodies, our parental instincts and the Lord's ability to speak to us. We have outsourced so much of our parenting to 'experts' that we struggle to confidently find our own rhythm marked by grace instead of worry. My friend Hermione told me that when she was pregnant with her first child she didn't read *anything* online about parenting because she wanted to trust in her own God-given ability to be a mother. The temptation to Google everything while pregnant is immense so the fact that she refrained from looking at message boards was startling to me. During an interview I held with her, she shared how reducing the amount of research was important for managing her expectations. This is what she said:

> Don't read too much, don't look into it too much. You were made to do what you're going to do. I was made to be a mum… I didn't read, I didn't look into it, I didn't ask questions. I did it and I loved it because I had no expectations.

Hermione's first pregnancy was out of wedlock, and she received a lot of criticism, but her conviction that she was made for this role allowed her to confidently enjoy her own experience of motherhood for what it was. To this day, three children later, I continue to admire the grace with which she navigates motherhood. God has entrusted our children to us, and the sad thing is that while the pressure of parenting is hardly their fault, they often bear the brunt. If we want to discover what an easy yoke looks like we need to courageously face some of the things that get in the way of us embracing the sufficiency of God's grace for us in this area.

Our own upbringing

No matter how many self-help books we read, the reality is that we parent out of who we are. Our children often trigger old feelings in us that were lying dormant before they arrived on the scene. Sometimes, they're positive but sometimes they're not and we don't know what to do with them. Psychotherapist Philippa Perry asserts that understanding our parenting journey starts with understanding how we've been parented. It shows up in the way we respond to our children and our expectations of them. 'If we don't look at how we were brought up, it can come back to bite us.'[11] Choosing not to work on ourselves as parents means that passing on the good, bad and ugly is inevitable. We can pray for generational cycles to be broken, but we also have to take a look in the mirror and work through our stuff. Sometimes that mirror is our children themselves. They start talking and acting like us and it's scary, especially if it's the parts of us we don't like!

Parenting has been one of the most triggering experiences for both Aaron and me. There are times when I read my child's experiences through my own and assume that they must feel in that moment as I did, but Perry asserts that if we feel discomfort when parenting we can choose to become more self-aware and understand if our responses are rooted in the past or a reaction to the present. Aaron has shared with me how as a parent he finds it easy to compartmentalise what the children need rather than looking at them holistically. A 'get the job done' mentality that says, *I'm not interested in how you're feeling*. We don't have to repeat our childhood in our own parenting or do what was done to us. Ultimately, this means that we don't end up holding our children responsible for our past pain. Aaron traced his behaviour back to the safety mechanism he used to protect his own heart growing up without a dad and as a professional sportsman. He can see the dysfunction of his upbringing and doesn't want to see it replicated. However, he recognises that even with the tools given, this desire has the ability to create pressure. If it's not rooted in faith, it's easy to lean on our own understanding and try to fight through our insecurities in our own strength.

The possibility of rewriting our story is inherent in our identity as children of God. We are new creations, reborn into his family with a spiritual inheritance. Our God is in the business of making things new and when we bring our challenges to him, he helps us find an alternative narrative. So how do we find new responses to the mantras increasing our pressure on parenting?

Through the eyes of a child

Even at their young ages our boys have taught me so much. Their little minds ask the most incredible questions and make some of the most profound statements. The disciples had been asking who would be the greatest of them in the kingdom and Jesus pointed them to the humility of a child. 'Truly I tell you, unless you change and become like little children, you will never enter the kingdom of heaven' (Matthew 18:3). It is easy to be dismissive of our children, but their innocence, simplicity, teachability and unworldliness points us to the kingdom. Here are a few lessons I've learnt from mine that I believe can help to take the pressure off parenting today.

Experience trumps price tag

One year we went on a family holiday to Dubai and the following year, on a glamping trip staying in a geodome. In Dubai we saw fancy malls, theme parks, stayed in plush hotels, went to the beach and ate nice food. Glamping, we did fire making, den building, ate pot noodles and caught frogs! They were both brilliant trips, just completely different locations with completely different price tags. When we asked the kids which holiday, they preferred they said they couldn't decide.

The trip to Dubai was probably ten times more expensive but the glamping trip equally memorable. Their response was a reminder that more important than the destination or cost is how much enjoyment we get out of it. The boys have spent more hours cutting, sticking and creating with cardboard boxes than they have with brand new toys. Rather than 'have more', what if we prioritised experiences and creativity? As well as leading us in the direction of sustainability, it definitely reduces the bottom line.

We all thrive off being empowered and empowering others

While we're feeling the pressure to prepare meals and breastfeed exclusively, our children are also feeling the pressure to 'be more'. Not so long ago my boys reminded me what truly matters. When my youngest AJ was a few weeks old, Jude and Israel came up with a phrase for him, which I caught on camera: 'AJ, you are smart, you are strong, you are brave and you are confident.' We have since printed this on posters and T-shirts and it has become a little mantra in our home. When they're feeling deficient, it's one of the things we say to remind them of who they are. Rather than trying to perfect and correct, what if we chose to speak life over our children *as well* as ourselves? As we challenge our own inner critic and the message that we aren't enough, we too have a much-needed reminder that even in our imperfection, God's grace is sufficient for us.

Presence and play communicates love more than anything else

In our excessive activity, we can squeeze out the simplicity of presence. One afternoon, we decided to randomly ask the kids how they knew we loved them, and the first thing Israel said was, 'Because you play with us.' As parents we work long hours so they can 'do more' but more than anything they love to play with *us*. Board games, sports, fishing, wrestling, crafts, dance, water fights whatever. Laughing and having fun together brings so much refreshing to our home and our hearts. The benefits of play and specifically undirected play are well documented for children and adults alike. Relationally, it helps to strengthen our bonds. By resisting the pressure of intensive parenting, we help to lead our children towards the life-giving values of presence, rest, unconditional love and the truth that we are not defined by what we do.

It's not always easy to be upbeat and optimistic about parenting. The thought of making changes alone may even signal pressure. Some days we have the strength to live our ideals but others we don't. Some parenting days are weighed with feelings of sadness and loss and amid all the joys that children can inevitably bring, we need room to process our more negative emotions too.

Key spiritual practice: Lament

In not wanting to overshadow the honour and joy of parenting, it can be difficult to talk about the times when we're finding it hard. Children are a blessing from the Lord but the many expectations about how we *should* feel in this area can create shame and leave us struggling in silence. Furthermore, because parenting consumes so much of our time and faculties, it can be difficult to find the mental and emotional space to process the disappointments and losses we experience through it too. Whether hoping to have a child one day, currently parenting or grieving a child, loss is something we can all relate to. Here are some examples of the losses we may experience:

Loss of child

Loss of our own parents

Loss of relationship

Loss of control

Loss of father or mother for our child

Loss of family unit

Loss of self-identity

Loss of our own childhood

Loss of freedom

Loss of mental wellbeing

Loss of finance

Loss of pre-pregnancy body

Loss of health

Loss of career

To lament is to cry out in grief. Although usually associated with death, through the Bible and the life of Jesus we can see how the spiritual discipline of lamenting allows us to express our deep sorrows to God, sometimes in nothing else but tears. Few things can impact us as deeply as our children do. Lament allows us to invite the Lord into the depth of our experience, rather than tempering our emotions in the shallow waters of optimism, which can result in us turning a blind eye to our issues, so as not to seem negative or lacking faith. If we are only able to speak and live from the place of the ideal, rather than the real, we are at risk of allowing our religion to not only silence us but paralyse us too. If, in all the rejoicing, declaring and dancing, we feel unable to mourn our unmet expect-ations and question the status quo, maybe we are more concerned with the opinions of others than the opinions of our heavenly Father, who wants to engage with our searching and sorrow?

I have often avoided stepping into this place for fear of being engulfed by my confessions, but this fear couldn't be further from the truth. In the Garden of Gethsemane, Jesus told his closest disciples that his soul was overwhelmed with sorrow to the point of death. According to Matthew, he asked his Father three times to take this cup from him before praying, 'May your will be done.' At Lazarus's death, he wept, even though he knew he had the power to raise him from the dead. The sounds of declarations and the promise of all things working for good fit neatly within my Pentecostal tradition, but what do you do when holding on to those words feels like trying to grasp the wind? We're often far more comfortable declaring victory and fixing things than acknowledging the mess – but the truth is, there's not always a happy ending and God has graced us for those times too. Our decision to lament isn't reflective of a lack of hope but gives us an opportunity to process our confusion and grief *with* hope because we recognise that we have a God who is concerned with our needs and we can cry out to him. Expression of any pain we have in relation to parenting opens the door to help, comfort and grace.

In music, major keys sound happy and light, whereas minor keys sound sad and melancholic. Bernard Anderson writes, 'Laments are really expressions of praise, offered in a minor key in the confidence that Yhwh is faithful and in anticipation of a new lease on life.'[12] Whether the song you're singing is in a major or minor key, you're still singing and that is enough. Holocaust survivor Elie Wiesel articulates how lament draws him closer to God amid deep and unanswerable faith questions: 'I have not lost faith in God. I have moments of anger and protest. Sometimes I've been closer to him for that reason.'[13] This sounds very much like what we read in the Psalms, the song book for the Israelites written thousands of years ago that continues to be treasured today – in part, for their honesty. One-third of them are laments and they remind us that God wants to hear our sad songs too. Sometimes they end in joyous praise, but sometimes they end in despair, like Psalm 120, a lament from start to finish.

We need to make room for the complexity of our humanity as parents – that's what grace does. Maybe you're navigating the sadness of childlessness, the trauma of a miscarriage, the disorientation of sleepless nights, postnatal depression, an overscheduled routine, the challenges of the teenage years, a longing for an end to youth violence, the growing mental health issues among our children or an empty nest now they're all grown. We may not have all the answers, but through our laments we affirm that God is with us in the triumphs and he's with us in the suffering too, gently leading us towards life, gently lifting the pressure off.

Let's take a pause and 'check in'. Look back at page 12 for some questions to help you reflect.

7

Pressure off power

In 2013 Aaron and I took a trip to Ghana, to visit some friends. During our stay we toured Elmina Castle, a major transatlantic slave hub in the central region. It was more harrowing than I imagined and what I didn't expect to see was a church located at the centre of this site of abject horror. While humans were chained like dogs, raped and left to die in their faeces, church bells were being rung and choruses raised right in the midst of it all. These 'believers' shrouded their evil with Christianity and their acts of violence continue to hinder the gospel today. It is a hard truth that in the pursuit of power there are no limits to what some will do, even with the Bible in hand.

In 2021 I chose to further my theological studies at the Queen's Foundation, home to the UK's first Centre for Black Theology. I had already been navigating issues of cultural inclusivity in my diverse church context but, in the aftermath of George Floyd's murder, this became a more urgent need. For the first time in my academic history, the majority of my lecturers and tutors were Black British scholars who were able to help me contextualise my experiences as a Black British woman seeking to follow Jesus. It was the first time my Black history was brought into critical dialogue with my faith. My first few lectures explored the enduring impact of colonial efforts to internalise a hatred of Africa (Afrophobia) and Blackness in order to cut people off from their roots so that they would be easier to control. They unpacked the impact of European colonisers who weaponised the Bible and projected a white hermeneutic to erase Black bodies from Scripture and justify their dehumanisation.

Colonial Christianity emphasised personal piety and sanctification while diminishing political engagement and liberation: freedom in Christ was a spiritual affair that did not concern the body. This even led to the printing of *The Slave Bible* which removed all references pertaining to freedom. In their book, *Faithful Antiracism*, Edmondson and Brennan write:

> The Society for the Conversion of Negro Slaves wanted to convert the enslaved people to Christianity without challenging the existing unjust economic and political systems that were crushing their lives and tearing apart their families. Missionaries 'adjusted' the Bible's message to accommodate the threats and pressure they received from economic and political systems. In other words, rather than fighting against injustice, they helped to sustain it using the name of Christ.[1]

Western philosophies were deemed superior to other indigenous epistemologies and many missionaries carried a Eurocentric bias of Christianity across the globe too. It wasn't just about power over people, land and policy but also power over knowledge.

As a British-born, second-generation Jamaican, my own mother has shared the feeling she had growing up that 'white was right' – and sadly this feeling about the supreme quality of whiteness continues today, even in our churches. It is perpetuated, sometimes subconsciously, by white leaders in their condescension and invalidation of the Black experience, their failure to recognise the importance of representation and their attempts to marginalise those who challenge the status quo. This can have the subtle effect of problematising Black people and subjugating them all over again if it goes unchecked. The churchgoers at Elmina had completely separated their worship of a loving God from their abuse of those created in his image. But how can such a compartmentalised view of the gospel be sustained?

The sacred and secular

You don't have to be in church long to realise that the pressure on power persists in similar ways to any other institution in society. We see our attempts to maintain personal power in small ways – like sitting in the same seat each week, or our attempts to increase social and structural power by climbing the ministry 'ladder', or seeking proximity to leaders. I've seen how people can feel intimidated by or afraid of church leaders, an honour culture that creates 'yes' people, and manipulation strategies that erode self-confidence. In faith communities, issues with power are particularly harmful because those who abuse it purport to have God on their side. This all works to distort people's reality and creates a fear of speaking out that allows the pressure on power to continue right under our nose. One of the reasons for this is that many of our Christian communities foster a culture that divides the secular and sacred. Anything that is not religious is devalued and even deemed dangerous or untrustworthy, while the opposite is true of those things concerning faith. So, studying your Bible is sacred, but going to university is secular. Listening to Christian music is sacred, but Hip Hop is secular. But what has this got to do with power today?

Many scholars have traced this dualistic thinking back to Plato and Greek mind-body philosophy which had a resurgence among evangelicals in response to the modern era. It is also seen in early Christianity through John's challenge to Gnosticism in the Bible. Promoting the belief that God is more interested in the spiritual than the material, visible life of the church, this posture creates a vacuum that has us heavy on the declarations and low on compassion, leading to passivity. When we feel *powerless*, a false contrast between the material and the spiritual can lead us to insulate ourselves from the pain and discomfort of our human experiences in a security bubble that lacks honesty and truth. Rather than prepare ourselves for the 'real world', we strive for a different reality that isn't right here right now but only speaks of the better that's coming. Our singing has upheld this escapism theology too: we sing about being on the other side of pain, as we should, but create little space for the sacred in the middle of life's chaos. We declare and prophesy those things as though they were, as we should, but then bury our heads in the sand. We speak of our unity in Christ, as we should, but we don't create space for the glorious diversity in which we have been created.

An overly-spiritualised, dualistic worldview anaesthetises us to the ills present in society, which is a convenient position for the privileged. It diminishes our sense of agency and exhausts our ability to care. In June 2017, Tim Farron resigned as leader of the Liberal Democrat party because he said that he couldn't reconcile being 'faithful to Christ' with being a party leader. Writing for Premier Christianity, he comments on the tension that exists between faith and politics.

Society assumes a separation between the serious business of the secular world and a supposedly private, disembodied faith. In reality, to be political is to care about how society is run and how people are treated. And the Bible is clear that God made every human being in his image, precious in his sight (Genesis 1:27). Therefore, it follows that he cares deeply about how we treat one another. The Bible is also clear that those who lead us are given their authority by him, and that they will be held accountable for their actions (Romans 13:1).[2]

Care is fundamental to Christian mission, so we *don't* have to fear engaging in the political world or addressing abuses of power among us. Doing so is a very natural outworking of a godly desire to respond to the needs of others. Following his way leads us to the conclusion that mission, and justice cannot be separated. It leads us to be curious about why things are the way they are and ask who has the power to change them.

An increased awareness and curiosity about injustices within the Church has contributed to the growth of deconstruction among millennials and Gen Z, as they seek to find better, more inclusive ways to follow Jesus. But addressing issues of power is never easy, particularly in faith communities where the line between professional and private relationships is often blurred. Andy Crouch reflects on his experience of a large, mega-style church where he asked the pastor how he handles the power that comes with his role. The pastor responded by saying there were no issues because 'We are all servant leaders here.' However, Crouch comments that this church, like many others:

> Assiduously cultivates an informal, low power distance mindset – the daily wardrobe in its corridors runs a narrow gamut from ripped jeans (on the youth workers) to khakis (on the senior pastor). But I have felt the change in atmosphere when this leader walks into a room. It's as if someone had abruptly turned down the thermostat and shut off the background music. He is a servant leader. But he is also a person with power.[3]

If we believe that power is not an issue that requires our attention, then it becomes more difficult to hold our leaders accountable.

So how do we begin to close the gap when historically our theology has maintained hierarchies of power and reproduced systems of oppression?

Toward biblical holism

The study of theology has been dominated by white, Western, male interpretations of the Bible that claim universal validity. Many scholars however, have now worked to develop contextual theologies that centre the existential realities of marginalised groups in dialogue with Scripture and tradition. Some argue that contextual theologies lead to a loss of orthodoxy, but in his book, *God and the Gangs*, Professor Robert Beckford states that paying attention to experience is avoided by traditionalists because they want to maintain what they call objectivity, which he argues is no objectivity at all.[4] He warns against 'dangerous, destructive and errant theological interpretations'. Similarly, Professor Esau McCaulley advocates for 'a model of interpretation that involves an ongoing conversation between the collective Black experience and the Bible'. McCaulley asserts that 'the Word of God speaks the final word', and that this needn't be in opposition to engaging the diversity of our human experiences. Instead, he encourages a 'hermeneutic of trust in which we are patient with the text in the belief that when interpreted properly it will bring a blessing and not a curse'.[5]

Black theology has highlighted Black presence in the Scriptures and taught a corrective historiography that revalues the contribution of Black people to the foundations of Christianity while also engaging their present story with the gospel. Similarly, Christian feminist theologies have re-examined the Scriptures to challenge practices that marginalise and disempower women. Black feminists and womanist theologians however have uniquely helped us to explore holistically the layered impact of marginalisation. Building on this work, lawyer and activist Kimberlé Crenshaw coined the term 'intersectionality' to talk about the way multiple identities such as disability, sexuality, gender, ethnicity, class, religion, etc lead to multiple forms of oppression. An awareness of the complexity of these lived experiences can help us grow in empathy and compassion for others, espcially when they are suffering.

My friend is a survivor of the Rwandan genocide and shared how having witnessed such brutality, even at the hands of religious leaders, brought into question what it means for God to love and have power – and seemingly withhold both. Having lived through this period of immense violence, it wasn't possible to settle for a surface reading of Old Testament stories about mass violence or interpretations offered by those removed from his story. Textbook theodicies won't do in the midst of our existential crises and, historically, they have shifted blame to the traumatised. So how might we holistically and meaningfully engage with feelings of powerlessness in the face of suffering and evil?

In *Bearing Witness*, Karen O'Donnell and Katie Cross discuss how trauma theology leads us to listen and bear witness to the pain of others, 'to feel God's presence and God's absence at the same time'.[6] Western Christianity has a tendency to rush from the despair of the crucifixion to the joy of the resurrection, estranging us from the confusion and suffering of a Holy Saturday, but this is often not faithful to the reality of our human experience. They share how paying attention to the different moments within the Easter narrative can help create room to engage with God's love in the midst of suffering. Developing a more holistic theology and practice requires us to wrestle with God as we centre the uncomfortable experiences of those who have been oppressed in order to meaningfully reimagine what it means to care and love.

It also requires us to understand our history.

Lest we forget

In 2007, as part of my secondary school teacher training, I visited Auschwitz, the largest Nazi concentration camp for Jews in Poland. It remains open to the public today in memory of those who were brutally slaughtered there, and as a reminder of our moral responsibility to resist genocide, prejudice and hatred. An accurate retelling of history helps us to understand how we have arrived at our present location. It helps us to learn so we can more intelligently begin.

I became a Christian within the Pentecostal tradition, which finds its roots in the Azusa Street revival of the early 1900s. Led by an African–American man called William Seymour, it attracted people of all races, genders and classes to experience an outpouring of the Holy Spirit, evidenced by gifts of the Spirit such as speaking in tongues and bodily healing. Seymour was the son of freed slaves and, in the midst of a segregated Jim Crow America, Azusa was marvelled at for its inclusivity and holism. Sadly, this transformation of social structures didn't last because many whites were unhappy about having a Black leader and wanted to practise segregation. This resulted in a split and eventually led to the birth of the Assemblies of God movement, of which I'm a part. Providing a compelling look at the trauma of Seymour and other Black Pentecostals, in dialogue with colonial theology, Dr Selina Stone writes:

> While Seymour and other early Pentecostals may have sought to avoid politics in order to focus on higher spiritual concerns, politics – and particularly the trauma of their political experience as Black people in America – could not be avoided even within the church.[7]

Stone explores the historic and continuing emphasis on personal piety alongside the absence of political engagement for Black Pentecostals today as a trauma response. In Black Pentecostal churches there tends to be an overemphasis on things that are deemed to be spiritual in contrast to their engagement with structures of power that inhibit their bodily, lived experiences. Tracing their story back to Azusa and foregrounding the significance of their struggles, Stone discusses why this might be. She then locates tools for Black healing and 'the restoration of a truly Pentecostal theology' within the holism of an African traditional spirituality, lost through the displacement of Black lives and at Azusa overshadowed by Western dualisms. Sometimes our present-day issues of power have deep roots that we have to go back and address if we are to experience true transformation. But how is power viewed in society today?

Power in the culture

A Viacom study analysed different types of power after engaging with 11,000 people, aged thirteen to fifty-three years old, in eight countries on six continents. The report stated that power was seen as 'largely personal, collaborative and beneficial to many'.[8] In other words, it is not always seen as negative; people with power can do great good. Rather than having a singular gatekeeper, power can also seen as a collective force of many leaders. It's a system that is responsive and flexible with the ability to influence something on a bigger scale. The study found that this collective power demands to see injustice fought immediately and, because of the global accessibility of things like social media, those who would otherwise be overlooked are now able to hold decision makers accountable. In a landscape where the voices of the people are empowered by the megaphone of the internet and mass communication is no longer top down, power is flowing to the grassroots, broadening the size of the decision-making table and effecting change.

The flip side of this collective power, however, is that the masses can move quickly, with little information – and information that is often based on hearsay. 'Crowd power can reclaim narratives and tell stories from a new point of view, but also "cancel" people and ideas,' the study says.[9] It's a double-edged sword. On the one hand, it creates accountability but it also creates self-censorship because people fear making mistakes and causing conflict.

While Western society may be rejecting the objectivity of religion in part because of its connection to abuses of power, in her book, *Why Trust the Bible?*, Amy Orr-Ewing explores the timeless significance of the Bible in light of cultural shifts. She asserts that in our postmodernist landscape, 'Western society has evolved and settled on a new ideology to give society meaning – this movement is one that prizes the experience of those on the receiving end of injustice; it defines humanity religiously along these lines.'[10] Speaking of identity politics, she argues that, today, 'Identity reigns over everything,' and that, 'This way of seeing the world is the fruit of the postmodern fascination with the dynamics of power.' As the Viacom study found, it also leads to division and reinforces dichotomies that pressurise people into taking sides and arguing across enemy lines rather than coming together in collaborative conversation. They may nod and agree so they don't rock the boat, but resentment bubbles under the surface.

Amy highlights how vocal the Bible is on issues of injustice, and Jesus' life reveals its ongoing significance to the challenges of our day. It has not lost its relevance, but there is no doubt that where the church's prophetic voice has been absent, social justice movements have filled the gap. However, without Jesus at the centre, it's hard not to feel like the attention on power is deepening our divisions. Seeing a virtue in this tension, broadcaster Justin Brierley writes:

> In the secular West our religious instincts continue to run deep, even if we can't name who or what we are praying to … we're all believers deep down. We all believe that good must conquer evil and that justice really matters.[11]

So, what other guidance might we find in the way of Jesus to address issues of power today?

The Good Shepherd

Jesus described himself as the Good Shepherd and this image has traditionally inspired the nature of spiritual care that seeks to embody God's love. Like much of our Western discourse, however, it typically has an individualistic slant, estranging it from conversations about justice. Theologian Emmanuel Lartey comments:

> For too long, pastoral care has been defined within the intrapsychic and interpersonal life of human beings. Ignored in this understanding are the structures of political and economic power that determine the norms and context for daily life. Social justice cannot be divorced from care since a just environment provides the resources that make care possible.[12]

When we recognise that care is about power, we are more inclined to explore the ways in which we can engage systemically to impact the lives of those we are shepherding. Taking the pressure off power can feel complex and overwhelming, but here are three simple ways I believe that Jesus leads us to respond: To speak up, to seek unity and to serve.

Speaking up

Jesus' example leads us to care, especially for the most oppressed in our society (Matthew 25:31–46). We see him take a stand for the vulnerable and speak healing over the bodies of the sick. He rebuked the money changers who were exploiting people in the temple, refused to be silenced by the authorities and used his voice to speak out against the hypocrisy of the Pharisees. In his inauguration speech just before stepping into ministry he declared:

> The Spirit of the Lord is on me, because he has anointed me to proclaim good news to the poor. He has sent me to proclaim freedom for the prisoners and recovery of sight for the blind, to set the oppressed free.
> (Luke 4:18–19)

It is clear how matters of justice and responsiveness to the marginalised are totally central to Jesus, and his life affirms the holistic work of the Spirit in salvation beyond personal piety. Writer Andy Crouch asserts:

Power is not given to benefit those who hold it. It is given for the flourishing of individuals, peoples, and the cosmos itself. Power's right use is especially important for the flourishing of the vulnerable, the members of the human family who most need others to use power well to survive and thrive: the young, the aged, the sick, and the dispossessed.[13]

Jesus leads us to administer our power for good in every dimension: personally, socially and structurally. To influence, to resource, to advocate and effect change in the lives of the oppressed – as he did. We are whole beings and attending to these issues validates our witness and commitment to love.

Seeking unity

Jesus' heartfelt prayer to the Father for unity is deeply challenging in our world today. He prayed:

I have given them the glory that you gave me, that they may be one as we are one – I in them and you in me – so that they may be brought to complete unity. Then the world may know that you sent me and have loved them even as you have loved me. (John 17:22–23)

Loving our neighbour is adjoined to loving the Lord as the highest command for Jesus and, in Matthew 18:15–17, he gives some clear step-by-step guidance for how to resolve disputes in a way that creates room for the possibility of healing and reconciliation. In the book, *The Speed of Trust*, Stephen Covey comments that, 'We judge ourselves by our intentions and others by their behaviour.'[14] Seeking unity requires us to graciously believe the best about others before rushing to conclusions.

Edmondson and Brennan share how communally engaging with the gifts of lament, confession and repentance can also help foster unity, by helping to deal with the brokenness in our lives and society.[15] In the Beatitudes, Jesus blesses the peacemakers. In Matthew 5:23–24, he exhorts us to deal with disagreements before we bring our gifts to the altar, so our disputes don't linger. And in Matthew 5:44, he encourages us to pray for our enemies. Nelson Mandela, former president of South Africa said, 'As I walked out the door toward the gate that would lead to my freedom, I knew if I didn't leave my bitterness and hatred behind, I'd still be in prison.'[16] The message of forgiveness is empowering for all because it helps us to guard our hearts. Although we can't control others, we always have a choice about how we will respond to injustice. We don't have to nor will we be able to confront every abuse of power, so it's important to know what battles the Lord has graced us to fight. He gives us the ability to take a stand and also shows us when it's time to shake the dust from our feet when hearts are too hard. Choosing the way of Jesus helps us to release the burden of what we have endured. It helps us to take back our power and it releases us to serve.

Key spiritual practice: Servanthood

Although he is God incarnate, Jesus didn't have a power complex. He could have turned the stone to bread, he didn't have to heal the ear of the Roman soldier, he didn't have to wash the feet of his disciples and he could have rejected the cross – but he chose to submit to the will of the Father. As Crouch aptly puts it, 'Power is not the opposite of servanthood. Rather servanthood is the very purpose of power.'[17] The disciples asked who would be positioned closest to him in heaven. In response, he taught them that the greatest among them would be the least (Luke 22:26). It would be their service not their status that would give them proximity to Christ.

Even though Jesus knew his death was unjust, he took to the cross. He was betrayed by his disciple who desired economic power at all costs and mocked with apparent irony by those who hated him: '"He saved others," they said, "but he can't save himself! He's the king of Israel! Let him come down now from the cross, and we will believe in him"' (Matthew 27:42). This was the critical moment. What would he do? The Jews were awaiting the Messiah who they thought would continue the legacy of King David and topple Rome, but they saw nothing of regard in a carpenter's boy who entered the city on a donkey. How could he be so lowly and yet still be the King?

Meanwhile, Jesus was teaching the disciples, 'Very truly I tell you, unless a kernel of wheat falls to the ground and dies, it remains only a single seed. But if it dies, it produces many seeds' (John 12:24). They were too limited in their understanding of power to know that his death was going to justify and empower the whole of humanity. His submission to the cross was far from passive; it gave way to the baptism of the Spirit in the book of Acts that saw thousands filled with the presence of God at Pentecost. Jesus encouraged, 'But you will receive *power* when the Holy Spirit comes on you; and you will be my witnesses in Jerusalem, and in all Judea and Samaria, and to the ends of the earth' (Acts 1:8, emphasis mine). His willingness to serve and return to the Father allowed his power to be extended beyond himself to all believers for the continuing work of the kingdom. This is not just evidenced through the gifts of the Spirit, but through the *fruit* of the Spirit also.

Paul encouraged the Philippians:

In your relationships with one another, have the same mindset as Christ Jesus: who, being in very nature God, did not consider equality with God something to be used to his own advantage; rather, he *made himself nothing* by taking the very *nature of a servant*, being made in human likeness. And being found in appearance as a man, *he humbled himself by becoming obedient to death* – even death on a cross! (Philippians 2:5–8, emphasis mine)

From his incarnation, he set aside his privilege, kingly status and power in order to put on flesh and suffer with us. Like the disciples, sometimes we don't understand what God is doing, but Holy Saturday reminds us that silence does not equal absence or inactivity. He is the Lord of the beginning, of the end and he is the Lord standing with us right in the middle. In his life, death, resurrection and ascension, Jesus levelled the playing field. There is no longer Jew, Greek, male, female, slave or free because the demographics of the day that denoted power and privilege are null and void in the kingdom through the unifying Spirit of grace.

Rather than climbing the proverbial ladder of success for our own self-importance, Jesus shows us that in the kingdom, power is not given so that we can be puffed up, but so we can empower others. The spiritual practice of servanthood leads us to make better choices for ourselves and our communities, thus facilitating the liberating message of Christ. As put by writer Katelyn Beaty, 'People exercising godly power are willing to give it up in the ways Jesus did. They know that their power is provisional, deriving from God, and intended to be given away, not hoarded.'[18] When Christ is the goal, we serve – and, in dying to ourselves, we produce a harvest. While the lure of power is self-seeking and a hindrance to the empowering work of the Spirit, the practice of servanthood enables Christ's life-giving power to be extended to all. Pressure off!

Let's take a pause and 'check in'. Look back at page 12 for some questions to help you reflect.

8

Pressure off prosperity

I took over my brother's paper round at 11, then at 13, I accepted a Saturday job at my mom's hair salon washing weaves and keeping the shop floor tidy. I looked forward to receiving the white envelope that contained around £20 cash along with the free hair services too! By 16, I was working in JD Sports celebrating my first electronic pay cheque. It felt *good* to use that hole in the wall. One day, during a visit to the bank, my personal advisor randomly offered me a £2,000 credit card. At eighteen, and on £3.01 an hour, I had no business having credit – but at the time I was excited by the idea of 'free' money. From the fluffy money boxes that I received as a child, I was lured into a relationship with my bank that was far too trusting. From a crazed shopping spree in Miami before relaxing on the beaches of Jamaica, to computers, cars and fancy gifts on finance, that card began a downward spiral of further borrowing that enabled me to live beyond my means.

When I was about twenty-one, a lady from Christians Against Poverty (CAP) visited me at my parents' house. I'd got in touch with them because, at this point, I was £12,000 in debt and unable to keep up with the correspondence or the payments. She asked if she could see my bills and out came the black bin liner full of unopened letters. By this point my credit score was ruined and it felt like all my payments were being absorbed in the high interest rates and late payment fees. The borrower is indeed a slave to the lender (Proverbs 22:7) and I was under pressure because my irresponsible spending habits had caught up with me. While other friends with more financial sense were buying houses on 0% mortgages, I was paying off debt. My only saving grace was that I wasn't afraid of hard work and by this point I was earning a decent salary for my age. CAP contacted all my creditors for me and organised my payments into something more sustainable. It would take years to clear those debts and for my credit score to be restored. It would take even longer to work through the roots of my relationship with money.

Our finances have an impact on every area of life, yet we receive little in the way of education about how to manage money and, unless you're versed in economics and/or politics, it can feel like a haze trying to get your head around talk of the economy in the news today. But all these decisions being made for us have such a huge effect on our day-to-day lives. As I write we are going through a cost-of-living crisis in the UK. An article in *The Guardian* from August 2022 reads: 'UK inflation to hit 18% as energy bills rocket.'[1] Inflation leads millions of families to experience an increase in debt and it is always the poorest who are most acutely impacted. Policy is not my competency, but you don't have to be Martin Lewis, Money Saving Expert, to see that something is broken.

We live in a culture where our bank balance too often determines our worth and where our identities are wrapped up in our designer wardrobes. We want to avoid financial lack and provide our families with the best, but the reality is that, according to the Joseph Rowntree Foundation, more than one in five of the UK population (22%) are in poverty, equating to 14.5 million people. This isn't about being unable to afford luxuries; 'poverty means not being able to heat your home, pay your rent, or buy the essentials for your children'.[2] It's sad to think that almost one in three children are living in these circumstances and this sharply increases in single-parent families. It's a reflection of rising inequalities everywhere.

According to the 2022 Credit Suisse Global Wealth Report, while the bottom half of the global population owns less than 1% of total wealth, the top 1% has 46% of all household assets.[3] Competition may be making some of us richer, but in the words of author and writer George Monbiot, we're falling apart.

> The war of every man against every man – competition and individualism, in other words – is the religion of our time, justified by a mythology of lone rangers, sole traders, self-starters, self-made men and women, going it alone. For the most social of creatures, who cannot prosper without love, there is no such thing as society, only heroic individualism. What counts is to win. The rest is collateral damage.[4]

But it seems that even our definition of what it means to win needs a revision, because where exactly are the true winners? The desire for more doesn't cease even when we are super rich, as this observation from *The Atlantic* magazine illustrates:

> A survey by Boston College of people with an average net worth of $78m found that they too were assailed by anxiety, dissatisfaction and loneliness. Many of them reported feeling financially insecure: to reach safe ground, they believed they would need, on average, about 25% more money.[5]

And if you've ever spent time with the poorest people, you will know that the capacity for joy doesn't cease with a reduction in material possessions either. In a 1968 election rally, Robert F. Kennedy wisely pointed out that GDP does not measure 'our wit nor our courage, neither our wisdom nor our learning, neither our compassion... it measures everything in short, except that which makes life worthwhile'.[6] We cannot deny that life necessitates the ability to create wealth but maybe it is indeed our neglect of measuring the 'worthwhile' that has sent us on this wild goose chase to nowhere? If the pursuit of success as defined by fame, wealth and power doesn't lead to fulfilment, then what does?

First things first

There are over 2,000 verses in the Bible about money. If that doesn't signal its importance, eleven of Jesus' thirty-nine parables spoke about the topic. He addressed it more frequently than heaven and hell and it's clear that his way flips our prevailing cultural disposition on the head. At the end of Matthew chapter 6, after sharing some strong words with the disciples about money and encouraging them not to worry about their material needs, Jesus tells them what to do in order to live with grace and without fear in the area of provision. He says, 'But seek first his kingdom and his righteousness, and all these things will be given to you as well. Therefore do not worry about tomorrow, for tomorrow will worry about itself. Each day has enough trouble of its own' (Matthew 6:33–34). But what does it mean to seek the kingdom and his righteousness? Let's break it down.

The word 'seek' according to Strong's Greek translation means to search for, desire, require, demand. 'First' is about the order of priority and a 'kingdom' is a territory over which a king rules. God's kingdom isn't a physical territory like an earthly kingdom, but in seeking the kingdom of God, we are desiring and demanding his rule and reign in our lives. Jesus also taught the disciples to pray, 'Let your kingdom come, let your will be done on earth as it is in heaven.'

As we pray, we are asking that our affairs and our world should come under God's authority and for his will to be done. The word 'righteousness' is a legal term that is about being in right standing with authority and Jesus is saying that we should desire to be in right standing with God. Because of sin, however, 'There is none righteous, no not one' (Romans 3:10). We have all fallen from this standard, so righteousness is not something we can strive for; it is gifted to us. 'God made him who had no sin to be sin for us, so that in him we might become the righteousness of God' (2 Corinthians 5:21).

Jesus fulfilled the righteous requirements of the law and in receiving him as our Saviour we have been justified.

Yet still, he taught, 'Blessed are those who hunger and thirst for righteousness, for they will be filled' (Matthew 5:6). From the security of knowing that we are fully loved and accepted by God, therefore, we also desire to live according to his way and his moral standards. 'But thanks be to God that, though you used to be slaves to sin, you have come to obey from your heart the pattern of teaching that has now claimed your allegiance' (Romans 6:17). This is not behavioural change but rather an obedience to Jesus' pattern of teaching that willingly flows from the heart now that we have been set free from sin. By grace alone we are now 'slaves to righteousness' (verse 18). A search for the kingdom and righteousness, then, is marked by a deep desire to obey and serve the Lord above all else, to pattern ourselves after him. It is a reflection of our continuing dependence and love beyond the miracle of salvation. And when it is our priority, he satisfies our yearnings in a way that the temporary fulfilment found in material things never can.

Treasure

Whether we're in debt or in plenty, if we've grown up with an unhealthy set of values and relationship with money it can be hard to shake. Money is not a sexy topic because it brings out all the skeletons in our closet. However, if we want to get serious about taking the pressure off prosperity, I think a great place to start is with our own story. Trying to understand what money values have been handed down to us is an important step. Thinking through what's worked, what hasn't and why, might help us make sense of our behaviours.

While I navigated my entry into the working world, my financial ideals were being shaped by the black box. As an aspiring musician I loved seeing my music idols showcase their lavish lifestyles on

MTV cribs; maybe one day that would be me. What I didn't know, however, is that for many of them, that wasn't their life either. Many of the houses in the show were rented, along with the cars and butlers to finish the facade. Talmon Joseph Smith for the *New York Times* writes:

> *Cribs* wasn't alone in manufacturing what's now called clout chasing. The decade it belonged to was flush with wealth worship, class striving and conspicuous consumption. MTV's *Pimp My Ride*, VH1's *The Fabulous Life of ...*, ABC's *Who Wants to Be a Millionaire* and NBC's *The Apprentice*, hosted by Donald J. Trump, are all indelible.[7]

These programmes helped to lure us into the trappings of what the Bible calls covetousness, an exhausting reality that feeds our discontentment, our greed and the belief that the grass is greener on the other side. They sold the lie that fame and money equals happiness and, with the rise of YouTube, these beliefs are trickling down to our children too. A recent study found that: 'British children no longer aspire to be train drivers or nurses – more than a fifth say they "just want to be rich": wealth and fame are the sole ambitions of 40% of those surveyed.'[8] So how do we begin to redefine these values that are so embedded within us?

Jesus knows how important money is for our survival and also how strong the lure of earthly wealth is. King Solomon said, 'Whoever loves money never has enough, whoever loves wealth is never satisfied with their income. This too is meaningless' (Ecclesiastes 5:10). Resource is not an issue for God, but our heart is. Continuing in Matthew 6, Jesus goes on to teach about storing treasure and explains 'For where your treasure is, there your heart will be also' (verse 21). In other words, whatever we treasure will attract our seeking. Rather than devoting our hearts and, subsequently, prioritising our time to storing up the treasure of material wealth, he tells us to store up our treasures in heaven, where he is. When Christ is our treasure, our hearts and our time are prioritised around living for his glory. This doesn't mean we won't enjoy life's pleasures, but it helps us to hold material things lightly. When our heart is invested in heaven, we aren't tired by the search or maintenance of earthly kingdoms and temporary accolades – unlike when money is on the throne.

A terrible master

If the pursuit of wealth is our devotion, it will at some point come into conflict with our pursuit of God. He desires our whole heart and he will not share it with anything or anyone else. Jesus continues to teach that, 'No one can serve two masters. Either you will hate the one and love the other, or you will be devoted to the one and despise the other. You cannot serve both God and Money' (verse 24). A slave is the property of their master and so is not able to respond to two masters with complete devotion. If the pursuit of God's kingdom is our endeavour, it will cause us to reject the pursuit of wealth at times. Matthew Henry explains:

> While two masters go together, a servant may follow them both; but when they part, you will see to which he belongs; he cannot love, and observe, and cleave to both as he should. If to the one, not to the other; either this or that must be comparatively hated and despised.[9]

Money is a great servant but a terrible master. Whether we have plenty or a little, it is the biggest cause of stress and corruption in the world. As our master it can cause us to be unwise, compromise our values and lead to the harmful treatment of others. For example, in recent times, fashion brand SHEIN appeared in a Channel 4 documentary revealing that their employees were working up to eighteen-hour days and only given one day a month off.[10] Exposure of these hidden practices can help to bring change in society but what about the pressures we're experiencing in the church?

The prosperity gospel

I became a Christian in 2002, during the height of what has been called the prosperity gospel – and I have numerous books to prove it! Originating in the US, theologian Dieudonné Tamfu describes it as:

> A perversion of the biblical gospel, according to which Jesus is a means to the blessings of health, wealth, and power. The preachers of this 'gospel' may quote God's word, but twist it to support their false theology. By taking passages out of context, applying a naively literal hermeneutic, embracing an over-realized eschatology, and misapplying their texts, prosperity preachers distort the Scriptures and exploit those who follow them.[11]

Whereas Jesus commands the disciples to seek God's kingdom first and not to worry, the prosperity gospel uses people's worries and the desire for prosperity as a motivation to give. For example, encouraging people to give in order to gain their own healing or debt cancellation. People may even be scared or manipulated into giving specific amounts to avoid being cursed. A friend shared that some years ago while attending a meeting he was so compelled to 'sow a seed' that he withdrew money at a high interest rate from the cashpoint so that he could give an offering on credit. At the time he believed that he wouldn't have been able to 'receive the word' otherwise, but now he can see how problematic his thinking was. In my own church we had a guest speaker who was supposedly giving prophetic words to the congregation. However, my pastor noticed that he was reading from the paper on which he had asked people to write information about themselves and passing it off as divine revelation! With hundreds gathered, my pastor courageously shut the meeting down. Yet some time later, I saw the same guy on TV inviting people to call in for their prophecy.

Riding on the back of Western individualism, the prosperity gospel is at its most stark in nations where there is abject poverty on the doorstep. It is perhaps most harmful in impoverished communities because its content minimises the suffering and oppression people endure often as a result of systemic issues like corrupt leadership. The Lausanne Movement completed a paper on this and wrote:

> We are also grieved to observe that Prosperity Teaching has stressed individual wealth and success, without the need for community accountability, and has thus actually damaged a traditional feature of African society, which was commitment to care within the extended family and wider social community.[12]

While rejecting a fatalistic attitude towards poverty and acknowledging the benefits that arise from empowering people towards hard work through use of their gifts, as the Bible does, the Lausanne Movement asserts that:

> We reject as dangerously contradictory to the sovereign grace of God, the notion that success in life is entirely due to our own striving, wrestling, negotiation, or cleverness. We reject those elements of Prosperity Teaching that are virtually identical to 'positive thinking' and other kinds of 'self-help' techniques.

It is true that many of the messages we hear in our churches today about wealth and being blessed sound almost identical to modern self-help language. Tamfu again:

When the passion for material things becomes god, God and his word become means. The movement dethrones Jesus so that his word becomes merely a manual for mammon, a guide to gold, a footpath to fitness, and a means to might. Ministry becomes business.[13]

The lavish lifestyles that often accompany those at the forefront become evidence of their blessing from God. It's understandable then that some people feel cautious giving to the church. How do we discern between the message of the kingdom and the message of mammon?

Knowing how much emphasis Jesus put on money, perhaps it should be unsurprising that the lure of wealth has diverted those who are seeking in many of our congregations too. The story of Jesus angrily overturning the money tables in the temple captures how offensive it is to the Lord that the idolatry of money should find its home in the place where people gather to worship. If the prosperity gospel creates a distorted consumerist understanding of the Christian faith, like any lie, it needs to be confronted with the truth. Tamfu argues that: 'The best way to challenge prosperity theology – and protect ourselves from it – is to teach Christ-centered biblical theology, which reorients our worldview and desires to cherish Jesus above all.' When we are truly captivated by Jesus, our love for him shifts the priority of our life from 'things'. But does that mean it's not God's will for us to prosper financially? Can those with material wealth still enter the kingdom?

Encounters with the rich

Jesus said, 'What good will it be for someone to gain the whole world, yet forfeit their soul? Or what can anyone give in exchange for their soul?' (Matthew 16:26). If this wasn't enough to warn them, Matthew later records that Jesus twice comments on how hard it is for a rich man to enter heaven. 'Again I tell you, it is easier for a camel to go through the eye of a needle than for someone who is rich to enter the kingdom of God' (Matthew 19:24). His message to the disciples was clear. If they wanted to pattern themselves after him, it would require them to deny themselves. This call was extended to the rich young ruler who had kept all the Commandments since he was young and wanted to know what he needed to do in order to inherit eternal life. Jesus responded to him saying, 'You still lack one thing. Sell everything you have and give to the poor, and you will have treasure in heaven. Then come, follow me' (Luke 18:22). The young ruler was saddened and rejected the invitation. His story reminds us that when Jesus challenges us to give, unlike the prosperity gospel, he doesn't promise financial gain on earth but a reward in heaven.

By contrast, in the following chapter, Luke records Jesus' interaction with another wealthy man, Zacchaeus the chief tax collector. Zacchaeus 'ran ahead and climbed a sycamore-fig tree' to see Jesus as he approached because he was too short to see over the crowds. I believe in this moment that he was seeking the kingdom. It is interesting that while the rich ruler attested to having kept all the Commandments, Zacchaeus was described as a sinner and Jesus' decision to enter his house shocked the community. What a statement! To be chosen by Jesus in front of all the people that despised him. Jesus didn't tell Zacchaeus what to do with his wealth,

But Zacchaeus stood up and said to the Lord, 'Look, Lord! Here and now I give half of my possessions to the poor, and if I have cheated anybody out of anything, I will pay back four times the amount.' Jesus said to him, 'Today salvation has come to this house, because this man, too, is a son of Abraham. For the Son of Man came to seek and to save the lost.'

(Luke 19:9–10)

Zacchaeus' desire for wealth was secondary to his desire for Jesus. Unlike the teaching espoused in the prosperity gospel, his salvation wasn't *because* of his giving, but rather it was his encounter with the Lord that led him to freely set the terms of his own generosity, unfocused on what he would get back in return.

But what about when we have bills to pay, mouths to feed? What is Jesus' response to a financial crisis? I had a conversation about this with my husband Aaron because for over a decade he has had a heart to resource the kingdom through the local church and to help people flourish in the area of finance. He has sat on boards to help navigate the need to fund ministry and has also put together courses to help disciple people in this area. He shared with me that because of our resource concerns, bite-size messages on tithing often dominate our conversations about money in the church. Conversely, steward-ship is often not talked about enough – for example, life insurance, money myths, childhood trauma, identity, debt, and so on. Instead, a give-and-you'll-get-back-and-be-fine narrative is emphasised to increase the offering size. This may be for a good cause or intention, but sometimes it's for selfish gain. He went on to say that true discipleship in the area of finance is about walking with people and giving them the practical tools to steward well and move away from a genie-in-a-bottle mindset concerning their finances. It's important to teach about delayed gratification and not having everything immediately, the value of leaving an inheritance for our children, and using the talents God has given to us. It is our duty of care, so that we are not only asking but also caring for people's wellbeing.

This becomes even more important in times of hardship, when people are likely to reduce the amount they give. Jesus' story of the poor widow (Mark 12:41–44), however, reveals that equal giving does not mean equal sacrifice. Two gifts that are the same size are not necessarily the same in God's eyes. When we reward people for their large donations, we inadvertently create a culture of pressure to match the giving of others whose situations and circumstances may be very different to our own. In doing so, we also fall into the sin of showing favouritism to the rich (James 2). Regardless of what we have, most people want to give and discipling them in the area of finance helps them to do this more freely.

Key spiritual practice: Generosity

When we moved to Manchester it took us a while to find our accommodation. There was a transition period which involved us heading back to Birmingham on a Sunday evening, but on one occasion we were in need of a hotel room. A lady from our church offered to let us stay in her house while she went away with her husband and son on holiday. She didn't know us, we'd never met, but she was happy to hand over her keys. I told her that I couldn't accept her offer but when it came to the crunch, we had no other option! When we arrived at the house, she had left food and refreshments for us and a lovely card inviting us to make ourselves at home in their bedroom. Her generosity changed our paradigm of giving. To pay for someone to stay in a hotel room – no problem – but to hand someone you have never met the keys to your house, that was a different level of generosity for us.

In the letter to the church at Corinth, Paul shared that the Macedonian churches were in 'extreme poverty' – but he also comments that they 'welled up in rich generosity' (2 Corinthians 8:2). Generosity isn't just about finance, it's a posture of the heart that says, 'Everything I have belongs to God and is available for his disposal.' The early church was not problem-free in the area of finance, but in the book of Acts we have an inspiring example of the power of generosity. 'All the believers were one in heart and mind. No one claimed that any of their possessions was their own, but they shared everything they had' (Acts 4:32). Here we see a thriving community that is working together to ensure the needs of everyone in it are being met. The description goes on:

There was no needy person among them. From time to time those who owned land or houses sold them, brought the money from the sales and put it at the apostles' feet, and it was distributed to anyone who had need.

(Acts 4:34–35)

Their treasure is no longer in earthly possessions, and they prioritise the health of the community over the wealth of an individual. This kind of communal giving can be seen today through initiatives like *Buhfai Tham* ('handful of rice') in north-east India, a modern-day example of the collective impact that giving a little can have.

The practice of generosity reminds us of our responsibility to care for each other and reinforces kingdom values. It's not guilt giving, which I for sure have done many times – but giving out of a genuine desire to share our life with others. Aaron also expressed the thought that when we give something away, we worry about what we are losing, but the Bible encourages us that it is more blessed to give than to receive. In fear, we may want to hold back our resources, our gifts, our time and talents but it's about having a vision greater than our own households that propels us to live generously with those who are less fortunate.

During the pandemic, we saw the rich ways in which generosity brought communities together, as people shopped for one another, took in relatives and friends, and suffered together. At times, when it feels like we are being squeezed financially, the natural thing to do is withdraw our generosity, but we receive and release grace when we share our life and resources with the right heart.

Generosity isn't performative and it's not about seeking approval from others. Jesus warned the disciples, 'Watch out! Don't do your good deeds publicly, *to be* admired by others, for you will lose the reward from your Father in heaven' (Matthew 6:1, emphasis mine). The motive of our giving has to be right. It is not to be performed and announced...

…with trumpets, as the hypocrites do in the synagogues and on the streets, to be honoured by others. Truly I tell you, they have received their reward in full. But when you give to the needy, do not let your left hand know what your right hand is doing, so that your giving may be in secret. Then your Father, who sees what is done in secret will reward you.
(Matthew 6:2–4)

Giving in private helps to protect the motives of our heart and prevent us from striving.

Jesus continues to teach that caring for the neediest is synonymous with ministering to him personally and that the kingdom of heaven is reserved for those who serve others in this way.

For I was hungry and you gave me something to eat, I was thirsty and you gave me something to drink, I was a stranger and you invited me in, I needed clothes and you clothed me, I was sick and you looked after me, I was in prison and you came to visit me.
(Matthew 25:35–36)

When grace enters our house, we don't have to be persuaded to give. When we understand what we have gained in Christ, giving is easy and motivated by a desire to minister to *him*. Our giving is no longer about the pressure to bring a tithe but the desire to share all that God has given to us. Paul declared:

But whatever were gains to me I now consider loss for the sake of Christ. What is more, I consider everything a loss because of the surpassing worth of knowing Christ Jesus my Lord, for whose sake I have lost all things. I consider them garbage, that I may gain Christ.
(Philippians 3:7–8)

The story of the sinful woman who washed Jesus' feet with her tears and hair, while anointing him with expensive perfume worth a year's salary captures this well (Luke 7:36–50). Jesus said that her lavish love was in response to the forgiveness she had received.

The truth is that no money can add to the joy of our salvation but, conversely, our salvation produces a flow of generosity in our life that adds immeasurable joy. Pressure off!

Let's take a pause and 'check in'. Look back at page 12 for some questions to help you reflect.

Conclusion: Pressure on

Whether it be the pressure to be productive or perfect, the pressures that come with our relationship status or the pressures that arise from power or money struggles, the saddest thing about succumbing to the unhealthy pressures in our world is the damage it does to our relationship with God, ourselves and each other. These pressures affect our ability to hear each other's hearts and be present; to walk slowly and to non-judgmentally disciple each other; to challenge injustice and prioritise care. We desperately need connection.

Without Christ's intervention the Bible is clear that humanity is hostile to God (Romans 8:7). We are alienated from him and others because of sin. In receiving his free gift of grace through faith, however, we are brought near and into friendship. We receive forgiveness, are reconciled and have the ability to live at peace with one another. This free gift doesn't mean we can be casual about how we live though. 'What shall we say, then? Shall we go on sinning so that grace may increase? By no means! We are those who have died to sin; how can we live in it any longer?' (Romans 6:1–2). To be a follower of Jesus means that I aspire to live my life a certain way. I may not be perfect but when I fall short of God's standard, it doesn't feel good. He is not just my Saviour, he is also *my Lord*, which means that I belong to him and choose to surrender to his will. Though this book has been all about taking unnecessary pressures *off*, it would be remiss of me to not conclude by talking about the one way we should desire to see the pressure *on*. Pressure bursts pipes, but when God's hand is involved, it is the kind of pressure that produces diamonds.

The heavy hand

In the few days leading up to preparing to speak at a women's event at my church in 2018, the Lord highlighted a passage of Scripture to me. I was reading through the Psalms one evening in my happy place – the bath – and though I had read the words of Psalm 32 before, I found myself reading them in a new light; it was as though they had been spoken from my own heart.

> Blessed is the one
>> whose transgressions are forgiven,
>> whose sins are covered.
> Blessed is the one
>> whose sin the LORD does not count against them
>> and in whose spirit is no deceit.
>
> When I kept silent,
>> my bones wasted away
>> through my groaning all day long.
> For day and night
>> *your hand was heavy on me*;
> my strength was sapped
>> as in the heat of summer.
>
> Then I acknowledged my sin to you
>> and did not cover up my iniquity.
> I said, 'I will confess
>> my transgressions to the LORD.'
> And you forgave
>> the guilt of my sin.
> (Psalm 32:1–5)

I was in awe of the Lord's timing once again and grateful for this revelation. This speaking engagement wasn't the first time I would be talking publicly about my abortion; I had told my story before and encountered women who shared the years of shame and emotional trauma they endured after their own terminations, often in secret. I had the opportunity to pray with them as they poured their heart out to God through floods of tears, just like my mentor Sandra had done for me many years ago. For some, it was the first time they'd told a soul and they were grateful for the opportunity to break their silence. I knew that pressure. In previous times, however, when I'd shared about the shame I once carried, learning to forgive myself, and the impact of my mentor, I'd never emphasised God's involvement in my story in this way before.

Lying in my bath, I had a strong sense that the Lord was highlighting to me that all the times I had felt alone before, during and after my abortion, his heavy hand was upon me, like a loving father, ushering me to repentance. When the Holy Spirit pricks our conscience, we may interpret it as condemnation and feel shame, but this heaviness of the Lord's hand is an act of grace to convict us of our sin. Shame disempowers and keeps us stuck, but godly conviction can help us acknowledge and positively move forward from past mistakes. Shame leaves you feeling like you constantly have to perform even though it will never be good enough. But, like a loving parent, God's pressure draws us into his presence to receive the grace he has provided through Jesus who has already put everything right.

While we recognise that, as believers, we are justified and no longer in the courtroom, knowing when we have committed a wrong is important. There is no condemnation, but Jesus did not come to do away with the law. The law was helpful for communicating God's standards and revealing sin, it just couldn't remedy the problem that it created. Therefore, the Lord applies pressure to bring us to a place of repentance and confession because, as pastor and author Rich Villodas writes, 'To repent is to acknow-ledge that a life turned away from God doesn't contribute to human flourishing.'[1] Exalting our shame above the finished work of the cross does not honour him, but receiving his grace does because it provides the help we need to live a transformed life.

The potter's hand

It was June 2016, ten months after our move to Manchester when I heard my pastor preach a message called 'Goo is Good'. She spoke about the life of the caterpillar and how to become a butterfly it has to completely lose form. It has to break down into what she called 'goo' in order to fulfil its destiny and evolve into the new. The cater-pillar's destiny wasn't to become a bigger caterpillar, it was to take on a whole new identity where it would no longer just crawl but fly. She shared this passage from Jeremiah.

This is the word that came to Jeremiah from the LORD: 'Go down to the potter's house, and there I will give you my message.' So I went down to the potter's house, and I saw him working at the wheel. But the pot he was shaping from the clay was marred in his hands; so the potter formed it into another pot, shaping it as seemed best to him.

Then the word of the LORD came to me. He said, 'Can I not do with you, Israel, as this potter does?' declares the LORD. '*Like clay in the hand of the potter*, so are you in my hand, Israel.' (Jeremiah 18:1–6, emphasis mine)

Listening to these words the Lord reminded me of a strange set of dreams I'd had years prior. He revealed to me that he was the one forming my vision and that in the process I was being moulded as clay in his hands. As the Potter applies pressure to the clay, it becomes formless and surrenders to a process that is quite frankly unpleasant. When that happens to us, it's painful to our pride and it challenges the very core of who we are, but we are being remade as he knows best.

The context of this passage is that the Israelites are in exile because of their disobedience. Exile was the worst thing that could have happened to them but they had persisted in their rebellion, despite God's forgiveness. In this passage, Jeremiah is delivering a prophetic word of hope. Although they are away from the Promised Land, he lets them know that they are still in God's hands. The encouragement for us today is that even when we go off track, the Lord still makes a way to restore us.

As the psalmist wrote in psalm 139:7–9, where can we flee from his presence? Even if we make a bed in hell, he is there, graciously leading us toward life. Sometimes we are fixated on the vision of what *we* want to do or be – but I'm constantly reminded that what God does in our life cannot be confined to our best-laid plans. Our identity is rooted in the person of Christ, and our purpose and destiny is rooted in his will for our lives. As passionate and as gifted as we may be, surrendering and allowing the Potter to form us as well as our dreams is important. He's forming us in his likeness. We can give birth to visions and ideas, but these things will come to life in the best possible way when he has shaped them.

The mighty hand

I've often felt ill-equipped and unqualified to fulfil the mission that God has given to me. Writing this book has often made me feel out of my depth and I frequently doubt my ability to speak, but as a disciple I recognise that an easy yoke doesn't equal the path of least resistance. Jesus chose the pressure of the cross for our redemption and he calls us to choose the kingdom above our comfort.

God wants to partner with us to carry out his mission on earth. Meeting Moses at the burning bush (Exodus 3), the Lord tells him that he has seen the oppression that the Israelites have been under at the hand of the Egyptians and that he has a plan to deliver them from slavery. He tells Moses to assemble the elders and go with them to the King of Egypt to request three days' release from their work to worship. Knowing that the king would not grant this, the Lord also says to Moses:

> But I know that the king of Egypt will not let you go unless a *mighty hand* compels him. So I will stretch out my hand and strike the Egyptians with all the wonders that I will perform among them. After that, he will let you go.
> (Exodus 3:19–20, emphasis mine)

Moses still doubted his ability to speak and was worried that the Egyptians would not believe him. God asked him what was in *his* hand. His staff would be the tool the Lord would use to set the people free and his brother Aaron would accompany him. Being called to oppose a world power and lead the deliverance of a nation must have been terrifying. The pressure was on, but Moses wasn't alone. It wasn't an instant victory, but in the end the Lord delivered Israel physically, politically and spiritually to worship. He even gave them favour with the Egyptians so that they didn't leave empty-handed (verse 21). They went with resources to sustain them.

Moses' willingness to humble himself under, and have faith in, the mighty hand of the Lord, in spite of his own inadequacies, meant that Israel would be liberated. Similarly, as Christians we are called to seek justice, sometimes in hostile situations. At times we will feel out of our depth, but throughout history God has raised up ordinary men and women who have courageously chosen to use what is in their hands. We can be those people today if we are willing, like them, to commune with the one who sends us.

The spiritual practices from which all others flow

Since walking in the cool of the day with Adam, God's desire has always been to dwell among his people, to live in *communion* with us. He gives us the power of choice and, even though it doesn't always produce the fruit that he desires, he doesn't take that freedom away because he gives us the freedom to choose. When he puts the *pressure on*, this is not the action of a power-hungry ruler wanting to control his creation, but the action of a loving father who wants what is best for his children and disciplines those he loves. He doesn't force our hand because he wants our heart. Our worship must be willing, or else it is not worship at all. Our giving must be willing, or else it's not generosity at all. Our obedience must be willing, or else it's not love at all. He is after a relationship, not religious duty and Jesus did what the letter of the law could not, he restored our ability for communion with the Father.

Before going to the cross, during Passover, Jesus instituted what we now know as the Lord's Supper.

And he took bread, gave thanks and broke it, and gave it to them, saying, 'This is my body given for you; do this in remembrance of me.'

In the same way, after the supper he took the cup, saying, 'This cup is the new covenant in my blood, which is poured out for you.'
(Luke 22:19–20)

Communion is an intimate time with the Lord – but also with one another. So much so, that we are required to put right any grievances with people beforehand. As we remember Jesus, the practice of communion is a place of *examination*, *surrender* and *decision*.

The pressure that comes from our pride and unwillingness to change can be crippling and difficult to admit but as we take communion we are reminded of Christ's lowliness, even to the point of death. We are humbled by the posture of the King who could have paraded his majesty, but instead chose to set aside his splendour for our salvation. From the wilderness, to Gethsemane, to the cross, he humbled himself for the joy that was before him, for *us*. In communion, we are reminded that we are deeply loved and, by grace, we are totally forgiven. Here we *examine* our hearts and confess our sins knowing that he is 'faithful and just … to purify us of all unrighteousness', so that 'times of refreshing may come from the Lord' (1 John 1:9, Acts 3:19). It reminds us of his heavy hand ushering us towards repentance, so that we are healed (James 5:16).

In communion, we also seek to mirror the Lord in our hearts. We may be tempted again but we are reminded that because of his grace, we can also come to him again and again and again. Sometimes the root of our dysfunctional behaviour is so deep that it takes time to see change. Sometimes God does things in a moment; at others, with the help of our trusted relationships, he patiently takes us on a journey of restoration that is equally miraculous and deeply formative. He loved us at the start, he's loving us in the middle, and he'll love us at the end. In communion, we *surrender* to the Potter's hand and, as he shapes us into his likeness, we are liberated to live in step with his ways.

Finally, communion reminds us that we are called out of our comfort to use the gifts and tools God has placed in our hands. To carry out the mission of God in the world. Not on our own, but together as co-labourers with him and our communities. Sometimes we are afraid and sometimes we face opposition, but we are not alone in our suffering. The world feels like an unsettling place, but this sacrament reconnects us with Christ's example of service and sacrifice in the face of hostility. His grace enables us to make the *decision* to courageously interact in the world carrying his love, presence, perspective and power – even when it's hard.

At a time of detraditionalization, communion reminds us that there are some traditions that are far too significant to abandon. The word 'Eucharist', as it is commonly known, in its Greek origins (*eucharistia*) means thanksgiving – and I am deeply grateful for this sacrament of love. The law that came through Moses was full of types, shadows and symbols, but the fullness of God, grace and truth came through Jesus Christ (John 1:17). Hallelujah! At the table we contemplate death, while his grace brings us together in confession and thanksgiving. We are pilgrims looking ahead to the joy of full communion with him and each other. The psalmist sings, 'Behold, how good and how pleasant it is when God's people live together in unity!' (Psalms 133:1). This is the purpose of *his* pressure – by grace it leads us on to the day when he will raise up these mortal bodies, renew the earth and unite us as one.

Pressure together

Whether it is journeying through life's pressures or leaning into the refining pressure of God, we are not designed to face any of it alone.

The Church – the *ekklesia* – the gathered community of believers (not the building) is God's great idea. It's the body of Christ and the bride he is returning for. In the UK, churches contribute millions of hours volunteering every month, meeting the needs of some of the most neglected in our society. Street Pastors, Christians Against Poverty (CAP), Common Sense, the Message Trust, Tearfund and First Class Foundation are just a few examples of charities tackling issues of justice on the ground and at the decision-making tables. The cooked meals, hospital visits, marriage counselling and prison ministry quietly happening in the background nurture our communities in immeasurable ways. I think of the artists, media platforms, teacher friends, lawyer friends and local government workers whose inspiration and service flow out of their faith and belief in human dignity. Our churches are the place where many of us have developed lifelong friendships, met our spouses, dedicated our babies and buried our loved ones and I'm so grateful for its existence. However, if the gospel is to be transformative, we have to be willing to critique the faith we have been handed down in light of the challenges of our time. To be brave enough to ask new questions without throwing the baby out with the bath water.

It is because of our love for the Lord and one another that I believe we should be passionate about addressing the false pressures that hinder our relationship with God and divide our hearts. Even if we struggle to attend a physical building, it's important not to forsake our gathering and to resist the temptation to casually break relations. I certainly don't advocate staying in toxic or abusive communities, but I believe it's important to attempt to work through things before walking away where possible. Sometimes, our periods of wrestling and staying when it's tough are the times when the most formative work is being done. The theologies that have us striving for a better reality somewhere 'out there' so we are unable to acknowledge the beauty and the valuable work the Lord is doing 'right here' in the midst of our chaos need to be challenged together. Life is messy. Accepting that makes it easier to enjoy each stage for what it is and to slow down without pressuring ourselves or those around us to be someone they're not.

As we have discussed throughout the pages of this book, sometimes the messaging we receive from our life experiences, society and even the church come into conflict with God's promise of grace through Christ. In a frenzied and fractured world, a commitment to authenticity, action and accountability can help us discern what is at work within us. In his popular book, *Atomic Habits*, writer James Clear said, 'Every action you take is a vote for the person you wish to become.'[2] Whether it's our health or our relationships, certain habits are required to maintain them over time. Likewise, spiritual practices help to sustain our spiritual life in the direction we have chosen. This means that sometimes we perform rituals and routines even when we don't feel like it. This isn't about religious duty, but an intentional commitment to being formed into the likeness of Christ.

And, finally, Jesus said that the entire law was summed up in these two Commandments: to love the Lord with all our hearts and to love our neighbours as ourselves. This is our greatest spiritual practice and, above all else, I pray that the words I have written will spur you on in this endeavour. To persevere through all the ways you experience pressure and to boldly lean into God so that you, those you cherish and those you are called to serve can live more freely, empowered by his extraordinary grace. A grace that invites us, always and irrevocably, into the hands of our loving God.

Notes

Introduction

1 'Results of the Mental Health Foundation's 2018 study', Mental Health Foundation (2018): https://www.mentalhealth.org.uk/explore-mental-health/mental-health-statistics/stress-statistics. 'Great Britain and Stress: How Bad Is It and Why Is It Happening?' FORTH (no date): https://www.forthwithlife.co.uk/blog/great-britain-and-stress.

2 'Mental health facts and statistics', Mind (June 2020): https://www.mind.org.uk/information-support/types-of-mental-health-problems/statistics-and-facts-about-mental-health/how-common-are-mental-health-problems. 'Mental health', World Health Organisation (2022): https://www.who.int/health-topics/mental-health. 'Mental Health of Children and Young People in England 2022', NHS (29 November 2022): https://digital.nhs.uk/data-and-information/publications/statistical/mental-health-of-children-and-young-people-in-england/2022-follow-up-to-the-2017-survey.

3 A. D. Botton, *Status Anxiety* (London: Penguin, 2005), p. 95.

4 'Religion, England and Wales: Census 2021', Office for National Statistics (2021): https://www.ons.gov.uk/peoplepopulationandcommunity/culturalidentity/religion/bulletins/religionenglandandwales/census2021.

5 'Modeling the Future of Religion in America', Pew Research Center (13 September 2022): https://www.pewresearch.org/religion/2022/09/13/modeling-the-future-of-religion-in-america.

6 H. Sherwood, 'Less Than Half of Britons Expected to Tick "Christian" in UK Census', *The Guardian* (20 March 2021): https://www.theguardian.com/uk-news/2021/mar/20/less-that-half-of-britons-expected-to-tick-christian-in-uk-census.

7 Hebrews 12:1.

8 B. Brown, *The Gifts of Imperfection: Let go of who you think you*

are supposed to be and embrace who you are (Minneapolis, MN: Hazelden, 2010).

9 D. Willard, *Renovation of the Heart: Putting on the character of Christ* (Colorado Springs, CO: NavPress, 2002).

10 James 2:14–26.

11 Luke 6:46.

12 Romans 12:2.

13 R. Villodas (27 March 2021): https://twitter.com/richvillodas/status/1375918691901186052?s=46&t=AG5dThsthwSUV-jcGk6OtA.

1 Pressure off productivity

1 C. Walker-Barnes, *Too Heavy a Yoke: Black women and the burden of strength* (Eugene, OR: Cascade Books, 2014).

2 F. DeBrabander, 'Should Work Be Passion, or Duty?' *New York Times* (2 September 2019): https://www.nytimes.com/2019/09/02/opinion/should-work-be-passion-or-duty.html.

3 D. Thompson, 'Workism Is Making Americans Miserable', *The Atlantic* (13 August 2019): https://www.theatlantic.com/ideas/archive/2019/02/religion-workism-making-americans-miserable/583441.

4 T. Morrison, 'The Work You Do, the Person You Are', *The New Yorker* (June 2017): https://www.newyorker.com/magazine/2017/06/05/toni-morrison-the-work-you-do-the-person-you-are.

5 J. Williams, *Climate Change Is Racist: Race, privilege and the struggle for climate justice* (London: Icon Books Ltd, 2021).

6 K. White, D. J. Hardisty and R. Habib, 'The Elusive Green Consumer', *Harvard Business Review* (July 2019): https://hbr.org/2019/07/the-elusive-green-consumer.

7 White, Hardisty and Habib, 'The Elusive Green Consumer'.

8 N. Klein, *On Fire: The burning case for a green new deal* (London: Penguin Books, 2019).

9 K. Beaty, *Celebrities for Jesus: How personas, platforms, and profits are hurting the church* (Grand Rapids, MI: Brazos Baker, 2022).

10 D. Wilkerson, Called to Be Christ-like, World Challenge (no date): https://www.worldchallenge.org/called-be-christ.

11 A. Lorde, *A Burst of Light: Essays* (Ithaca, NY: Firebrand Books, 1988).

12 P. Scazzero (27 September 2022): https://twitter.com/petescazzero/
status/1574763860590034944.

13 J. M. Comer, *The Ruthless Elimination of Hurry: How to stay
emotionally healthy and spiritually alive in the chaos of our modern
world* (Hodder & Stoughton, 2019).

14 H. Hudson (dir), *Chariots of Fire* (20th Century Fox, 1981).

2 Pressure off perfectionism

1 Brown, *The Gifts of Imperfection*.

2 'John Boyega Is on His Own Hero's Journey', Hypebeast
(9 December 2019): https://hypebeast.com/2019/12/
john-boyega-star-wars-rise-of-skywalker-interview-cover.

3 T. Curran and A. P. Hill, 'Perfectionism Is Increasing over Time:
A meta-analysis of birth cohort differences from 1989 to 2016',
Psychological Bulletin (2019), 145(4), pp. 410–429: https://doi.
org/10.1037/bul0000138.

4 T. Curran, 'Breaking Up with Perfectionism', TED (3
May 2022): https://www.ted.com/podcasts/worklife/
breaking-up-with-perfectionism-transcript.

5 Curran, 'Breaking Up with Perfectionism'.

6 J. Piper, 'Christian Identity and Christian Destiny', Desiring
God (17 April 1994): https://www.desiringgod.org/messages/
christian-identity-and-christian-destiny.

7 A. Kenny, *My Body Is Not a Prayer Request: Disability justice in
the Church* (Grand Rapids, MI: Brazos Press, a division of Baker
Publishing Group, 2020).

8 F. Godsden, interview with the author.

9 C. S. Lewis, *Mere Christianity* (London: Bles, 1952). *Mere Christianity*
by CS Lewis © copyright 1942, 1943, 1944, 1952 CS Lewis Pte Ltd.
Extract used with permission.

10 T. J. Keller, *The Freedom of Self-forgetfulness: The path to true
Christian joy* (Farington: 10Publishing, 2014).

3 Pressure off singleness

1 J. B. Smith, *Party of One: Truth, longing, and the subtle art of singleness*
(Nashville, TN: Nelson Books, an imprint of Thomas Nelson, 2018).

2 'The Research', *Single Friendly Church* (2012): https://www.singlefriendlychurch.com/research/research.

3 Lauren Windle, *Notes on Love: Being single and dating in a marriage obsessed church* (London: SPCK, 2021).

4 Regan Olsson, 'What Is Love Bombing and How to Recognize the Signs', Banner Health (23 September 2022): https://www.bannerhealth.com/healthcareblog/teach-me/what-is-love-bombing-and-how-to-recognize-the-signs.

5 Red Cross, 'Get Help with Loneliness': https://www.redcross.org.uk/get-help/get-help-with-loneliness.

6 N. Gill, 'Loneliness: A silent plague that is hurting young people most', *The Guardian* (20 July 2014): https://www.theguardian.com/lifeandstyle/2014/jul/20/loneliness-britains-silent-plague-hurts-young-people-most.

4 Pressure off purity

1 E. Thwaites, 'The Impact of Christian Purity Culture Is Still Being Felt – Including in Britain', The Conversation (28 June 2022): https://theconversation.com/the-impact-of-christian-purity-culture-is-still-being-felt-including-in-britain-182907.

2 J. Harris, *I Kissed Dating Goodbye* (Sisters, OR: Multnomah Books, 1997).

3 S. Bonne (5 July 2015): https://www.instagram.com/shannon.bonne.

4 Soul ties are the deep spiritual connection or bond between two people – they are discussed most prominently, although not exclusively, in relation to intercourse.

5 C. Benbow, *Red Lip Theology* (New York: Convergent Books, 2022).

6 Quoted in A. Robb, 'What It's Like Growing Up in the Evangelical Purity Movement', *Elle* (11 September 2018): https://www.elle.com/culture/books/a23080420/growing-up-evangelical-purity-movement-linda-kay-klein-pure.

7 Robb, 'What It's Like Growing Up in the Evangelical Purity Movement'.

8 After completing a diploma in sexology, Hannah Tarbuck now explores healthy sexuality over at https://themissionaryposition.co.uk.

5 Pressure off marriage

1 H. Hoffower, '7 Ways Millennials Are Changing Marriage, from Signing Prenups to Staying Together Longer Than Past Generations', Insider (2019): https://www.businessinsider.com/how-millennials-are-changing-marriage-divorce-weddings-prenups-2019-5?r=US&IR=T#millennials-are-fueling-a-declining-divorce-rate-1.

2 Z. Burke, 'How Much Does a Wedding Cost? The UK average revealed', Hitched (2022): https://www.hitched.co.uk/wedding-planning/organising-and-planning/the-average-wedding-cost-in-the-uk-revealed.

3 https://www.hitched.co.uk/wedding-planning/organising-and-planning/average-uk-wedding.

4 S. Kendrick and A. Kendrick, *The Love Dare* (Nashville, TN: B&H Publishing Group, 2013).

5 D. Bonhoeffer, *Letters and Papers from Prison* (New York: Macmillan Company, 1967).

6 N. Pearcey, *Love Thy Body: Answering hard questions about life and sexuality* (Grand Rapids, MI: Baker Books, 2019).

6 Pressure off parenting

1 J. Senior, 'The Crisis of Modern Parenting', TED (21 March 2014): https://blog.ted.com/the-crisis-of-modern-parenting-jennifer-senior-at-ted2014.

2 C. C. Miller, 'The Relentlessness of Modern Parenting', *New York Times* (25 December 2018): https://www.nytimes.com/2018/12/25/upshot/the-relentlessness-of-modern-parenting.html.

3 Senior, 'The Crisis of Modern Parenting'.

4 Miller, 'The Relentlessness of Modern Parenting'.

5 J. Lythcott-Haims, 'How to Raise Successful Kids – Without Overparenting', TED (7 November 2017): https://www.ted.com/speakers/julie_lythcott_haims.

6 Miller, 'The Relentlessness of Modern Parenting'.

7 A. Topping, 'Nursery for Under-twos Costs Parents in England 65% of Wage', *The Guardian* (7 October 2022): https://amp.theguardian.com/money/2022/oct/07/nursery-under-twos-costs-parents-england-65-percent-wage.

8 T. Chandola, 'Working Mothers up to 40% More Stressed, Study Finds', University of Manchester (28 January 2019): https://www.manchester. ac.uk/discover/news/working-mothers-up-to-40-more-stressed.

9 'March of the Mummies Demands', Pregnant Then Screwed: https:// pregnantthenscrewed.com/march-of-the-mummies-demands.

10 Salary.com, 'How Much IS a Mother Really Worth?' (2019): https:// www.salary.com/articles/mother-salary.

11 P. Perry, *The Book You Wish Your Parents Had Read (and Your Children Will Be Glad That You Did)* (New York: Pamela Dorman Books Life, 2020).

12 B. W. Anderson, *Out of the Depths: The Psalms speak for us today* (Louisville, KY: Westminster John Knox Press, 1983).

13 Quoted in J. Berger, 'Man in the News; Witness to Evil: Eliezer Weisel', *New York Times* (15 October 1986): https://www.nytimes. com/1986/10/15/world/man-in-the-news-witness-to-evil-eliezer-weisel.html.

7 Pressure off power

1 C. Edmondson and C. Brennan, *Faithful Antiracism: Moving past talk to systemic change* (Downers Grove, IL, InterVarsity Press, 2022).

2 T. Farron, 'There's No Separation between Faith and Politics', *Premier Christianity* (23 June 2022): https://www.premierchristianity.com/ opinion/theres-no-separation-between-faith-and-politics/13303.article.

3 A. Crouch, 'It's Time to Talk about Power', *Christianity Today* (1 October 2013): https://www.christianitytoday.com/ct/2013/october/ andy-crouch-its-time-to-talk-about-power.html.

4 R. Beckford, *God and the Gangs* (London: Darton, Longman & Todd, 2004).

5 E. McCaulley, *Reading While Black* (Illinois: IVP, 2020).

6 K. Cross and K. O'Donnell (eds), *Bearing Witness: Intersectional Perspectives on Trauma Theology* (London: SCM Press, 2022).

7 S. Stone in Cross and O'Donnell, *Bearing Witness*.

8 Velocity, 'Power in Progress: A Viacom velocity study' (2019), YouTube: https://www.youtube.com/watch?v=lX3PQwj9coc.

9 Velocity, 'Power in Progress'.

10 A. Orr-Ewing, *Why Trust the Bible? Answers to ten tough questions* (Nottingham: IVP, 2020).

11 J. Brierley, 'Less Than Half of UK People Now Identify as Christian – But the Christian story is far from over', *Premier Unbelievable?* (30 November 2022): https://www.premierunbelievable.com/articles/less-than-half-of-uk-people-now-identify-as-christian-but-the-christian-story-is-far-from-over/14403.article.

12 E. Lartey, *In Living Color: An intercultural approach to pastoral care and counselling* (London and New York: Jessica Kingsley Publishers, 2003).

13 Crouch, 'It's Time to Talk about Power'.

14 S. M. R. Covey, S. R. Covey and R. R. Merrill, *The Speed of Trust: The one thing that changes everything* (New York: Free Press, 2018).

15 Edmondson and Brennan, *Faithful Antiracism*.

16 N. Mandela, *Long Walk to Freedom* (Boston, MA: Little, Brown and Co., 1994).

17 Crouch, 'It's Time to Talk about Power'.

18 Beaty, *Celebrities for Jesus*.

8 Pressure off prosperity

1 G. Weardon, 'UK Inflation to Hit 18% as Energy Bills Rocket', *The Guardian* (22 August 2022).

2 'What Is Poverty?' Joseph Rowntree Foundation: https://www.jrf.org.uk/our-work/what-is-poverty.

3 'Why Wealth Matters: The Global Wealth Report', Credit Suisse (2022): https://www.credit-suisse.com/about-us/en/reports-research/global-wealth-report.html.

4 G. Monbiot, 'Falling Apart' (14 October 2014): https://www.monbiot.com/2014/10/14/falling-apart.

5 Quoted in Monbiot, 'Falling Apart'.

6 Robert F. Kennedy, Speech, University of Kansas (18 March 1968).

7 T. J. Smith, 'How "MTV Cribs" Rewired My Brain, and Maybe Yours Too', *New York Times* (26 August 2020): https://www.nytimes.com/2020/08/26/arts/television/mtv-cribs-mariah-carey.html.

8 Monbiot, 'Falling Apart'.

9 Available at: https://www.biblestudytools.com/commentaries/
matthew-henry-complete/matthew/6.html.

10 Channel 4 (17 October 2022), *UNTOLD: Inside the Shein machine.*

11 D. Tamfu, 'The Gods of the Prosperity Gospel', Desiring God
(4 February 2020): https://www.desiringgod.org/articles/
the-gods-of-the-prosperity-gospel.

12 Lausanne Theology Working Group, 'A Statement on the Prosperity
Gospel', Lausanne Movement (no date): https://lausanne.org/
content/a-statement-on-the-prosperity-gospel.

13 Tamfu, 'The Gods of the Prosperity Gospel'.

Conclusion

1 R. Villodas, 'The Wisdom of Ashes: Understanding Ash Wednesday',
Missio Alliance (1 March 2017): https://www.missioalliance.org/
wisdom-ashes-understanding-ash-wednesday.

2 J. Clear, *Atomic Habits* (Random House, 2018).